MW01244123

Pigskinizations

Books by LOUIS DANIEL BRODSKY

Poetry

Five Facets of Myself (1967)* (1995)

The Easy Philosopher (1967)* (1995)

"A Hard Coming of It" and Other Poems (1967)* (1995)

The Foul Rag-and-Bone Shop (1967)* (1969, exp.)* (1995, exp.)

Points in Time (1971)* (1995) (1996)

Taking the Back Road Home (1972)* (1997) (2000)

Trip to Tipton and Other Compulsions (1973)* (1997)

"The Talking Machine" and Other Poems (1974)* (1997)

Tiffany Shade (1974)* (1997)

Trilogy: A Birth Cycle (1974) (1998)

Cold Companionable Streams (1975)* (1999)

Monday's Child (1975) (1998)

Preparing for Incarnations (1975)* (1976, exp.) (1999) (1999, exp.)

The Kingdom of Gewgaw (1976) (2000)

Point of Americas II (1976) (1998)

La Preciosa (1977) (2001)

Stranded in the Land of Transients (1978) (2000)

The Uncelebrated Ceremony of Pants-Factory Fatso (1978) (2001)

Birds in Passage (1980) (2001)

Résumé of a Scrapegoat (1980) (2001)

Mississippi Vistas: Volume One of *A Mississippi Trilogy* (1983) (1990)

You Can't Go Back, Exactly (1988, two eds.) (1989) (2003, exp.)

The Thorough Earth (1989)

Four and Twenty Blackbirds Soaring (1989)

Falling from Heaven: Holocaust Poems of a Jew and a Gentile
   (with William Heyen) (1991)

Forever, for Now: Poems for a Later Love (1991)

Mistress Mississippi: Volume Three of *A Mississippi Trilogy* (1992)

A Gleam in the Eye: Poems for a First Baby (1992)

Gestapo Crows: Holocaust Poems (1992)

The Capital Café: Poems of Redneck, U.S.A. (1993)

Disappearing in Mississippi Latitudes: Volume Two of *A Mississippi Trilogy* (1994)

A Mississippi Trilogy: A Poetic Saga of the South (1995)*

Paper-Whites for Lady Jane: Poems of a Midlife Love Affair (1995)

The Complete Poems of Louis Daniel Brodsky: Volume One, 1963–1967
   (edited by Sheri L. Vandermolen) (1996)

Three Early Books of Poems by Louis Daniel Brodsky, 1967–1969: *The Easy Philosopher*,
   "A Hard Coming of It" and Other Poems, and *The Foul Rag-and-Bone Shop*
   (edited by Sheri L. Vandermolen) (1997)

The Eleventh Lost Tribe: Poems of the Holocaust   (1998)

Toward the Torah, Soaring: Poems of the Renascence of Faith   (1998)

Voice Within the Void: Poems of *Homo supinus*   (2000)

Rabbi Auschwitz: Poems Touching the Shoah   (2000)*

The Swastika Clock: Endlösung Poems   (2001)*

Shadow War: A Poetic Chronicle of September 11 and Beyond, Volume One   (2001) (2004)

The Complete Poems of Louis Daniel Brodsky: Volume Two, 1967–1976
   (edited by Sheri L. Vandermolen)   (2002)

Shadow War: A Poetic Chronicle of September 11 and Beyond, Volume Two   (2002) (2004)

Shadow War: A Poetic Chronicle of September 11 and Beyond, Volume Three   (2002) (2004)

Shadow War: A Poetic Chronicle of September 11 and Beyond, Volume Four   (2002) (2004)

Shadow War: A Poetic Chronicle of September 11 and Beyond, Volume Five   (2002) (2004)

Heavenward   (2003)

Regime Change: Poems of America's Showdown with Iraq, Volume One   (2003)*

Regime Change: Poems of America's Showdown with Iraq, Volume Two   (2003)*

Regime Change: Poems of America's Showdown with Iraq, Volume Three   (2003)*

The Complete Poems of Louis Daniel Brodsky: Volume Three, 1976–1980
   (edited by Sheri L. Vandermolen)   (2004)

Bibliography *(coedited with Robert Hamblin)*

Selections from the William Faulkner Collection of Louis Daniel Brodsky:
   A Descriptive Catalogue   (1979)

Faulkner: A Comprehensive Guide to the Brodsky Collection
      Volume I: The Biobibliography   (1982)
      Volume II: The Letters   (1984)
      Volume III: *The De Gaulle Story*   (1984)
      Volume IV: *Battle Cry*   (1985)
      Volume V: Manuscripts and Documents   (1989)

Country Lawyer and Other Stories for the Screen by William Faulkner   (1987)

Stallion Road: A Screenplay by William Faulkner   (1989)

Biography

William Faulkner, Life Glimpses   (1990)

Fiction

Between Grief and Nothing *(novel)*   (1964)*

Between the Heron and the Wren *(novel)*   (1965)*

"Dink Phlager's Alligator" and Other Stories   (1966)*

The Drift of Things *(novel)*   (1966)*

Vineyard's Toys *(novel)*   (1967)*

The Bindle Stiffs *(novel)*   (1968)*

Yellow Bricks *(short fictions)* (1999)
Catchin' the Drift o' the Draft *(short fictions)* (1999)
This Here's a Merica *(short fictions)* (1999)
Leaky Tubs *(short fictions)* (2001)
Rated Xmas *(short fictions)* (2003)
Nuts to You! *(short fictions)* (2004)
Pigskinizations *(short fictions)* (2005)

Memoir

The Adventures of the Night Riders, Better Known as the Terrible Trio
 (with Richard Milsten) (1961)*

Pigskinizations

Short fictions
by

L.D. Brodsky

TIME BEING BOOKS
POETRY IN SIGHT AND SOUND

An imprint of Time Being Press
St. Louis, Missouri

Time Being Books®
10411 Clayton Road
St. Louis, Missouri 63131

Time Being Books® is an imprint of Time Being Press®, St. Louis, Missouri.

Time Being Press® is a 501(c)(3) not-for-profit corporation.

Time Being Books® volumes are printed on acid-free paper, and binding materials are chosen for strength and durability.

The characters and events portrayed in these stories are fictitious. Any similarities to real persons, living or dead, is purely coincidental and not intended by the author.

ISBN 1-56809-072-2 (Paperback)

Library of Congress Cataloging-in-Publication Data:

Brodsky, Louis Daniel.
    Pigskinizations : short fictions / by L.D. Brodsky.— 1st ed.
      p. cm.
    ISBN 1-56809-072-2 (pbk. : acid-free paper)
     I. Title.
  PS3552.R623 P54 2005
  813'.54—dc22

                                 2005015295

Book design, typesetting, and cover photo by Sheri Vandermolen
Manufactured in the United States of America

First Edition, first printing (2005)

Acknowledgments

Once again, Jerry Call and Sheri Vandermolen, my editors at Time Being Books, have collaborated with me in enhancing the quality of my short fictions. Without their oversight and oversights, I would seem a damn sight stupider. Alas, they alone are responsible for all my mistakes.

For Jerry Call and Sheri Vandermolen,

who play Sergeant Hulka and Nurse Ratched
to the John Winger and R. P. McMurphy in me:

thanks, guys, for reminding me
that one absurdity is worth a thousand words.

Contents

Pigskinizations

Missing

You awaken in a cold sweat, jump from your wet sheets, in a frenzy — you need to relieve your bladder badly — grope for the light switch, then walk, at a brisk clip, past the armoire, glimpsing your naked physique in the full-length mirror, reach your bathroom barely in time to keep from pissing up your carpet. As it is, you spritz the bowl and both your legs.

For what seems a century, at least a minute, you hover over your American Standard, flicking your dribbling dick until it quits dripping; then you blot its head with toilet paper, to make sure you've done the trick. You pull three more sheets from the roll and fastidiously wipe off your legs and feet, before spinning on your heels, heading back to bed, for a few more hours of rest.

Out of creaturely habit, you turn off the switch you forgot, in your haste, to flip on in the first place. A cluster of sixty-watt bulbs explodes like a grenade. You squint, grasp the pain hammering your temples, cut the lights, with lurching urgency, shut the door behind you, for finality's sake.

But as you pass the armoire's man-high mirror, you realize your naked reflection is missing.

For the next three hours, you toss from side to side, lie prone, supine. Nothing in your darkness enlightens the mystery. Sleep and dreams refuse to do your bidding. Meditation and rumination fail you miserably, until gnawing curiosity finally tugs you from bed, makes you flick the switch again, confront the armoire. The mirror is still empty. You stare at yourself with invisible mortification.

The Ghost of Post-Thanksgiving

Heading to breakfast, then the office, this chilly Friday morning, he navigates the lanes with ease (the highway he usually starts and stops on, for the better part of an hour, is as brisk as the Mississippi at flood stage) and avidly listens to the news, which consists of statistics, strictly statistics.

On the way to his favorite café, he hears a reporter taking herself exceedingly seriously, as if her information were tantamount to that provided by the resident meteorologist or number-cruncher/stockbroker/analyst, responsible for keeping his ear to the S&P's track, his finger on the NASDAQ's vena cavae, his trouser worm on the thirty goddesses of the Dow . . . a too-buoyant local reporter for NPR, obviously not a tryptophan victim of the just-concluded Turkey/Dressing/Giblet Gravy Wars, who warns not of gridlock on the city's thoroughfares but rather on the parking lot of Target, which, at 6:28, is 75 percent filled, while, at Wal-Mart, 90 percent of the spaces are taken, with Penney's and Sears lagging at 50 percent. "But," she cautions with broadcast-school histrionics, "It's just a matter of time. By 7:15, there won't be any open patch of blacktop showing."

Next, her national counterpart details how plastic will be today's poison of choice, that, across the country, every single second, from cain't see to cain't see, 7000 credit cards will flash through scanners and that, come Christmas day, every perpetrator in the holiday-gift-giving scam — America's raping, pillaging, and plundering — will be in debt, on average, to the tune of a wilted $1200 bill, which will take 95 percent of the debtors, on average, a year and a half to pay back, at an average interest rate of 18 percent, compounded daily, which translates into a finance charge of $324, he breathlessly concludes, as if wrapping up a blow-by-blow description of the burning of the *Hindenburg*, the fight of the century, between Joe Louis and Max Schmeling, or those epiphanic events of two millenniums ago — the Crucifixion, Deposition, and Resurrection of Jesus — gasping, choking, about to break into public-radio tears.

"Jesus! Jesus!" he groans, traveling down the empty highway, to his favorite café. He has no problem parking on the lot. The skeleton crew of waitresses belongs to him alone. He eats his egg whites in joyous silence — a post-Thanksgiving ghost, who has no desire to haunt the Christmas season — and revels in his benign misanthropy.

The Perfect Marriage

She went around, night and day, unself-consciously wearing a clothespin on her nose. He returned, every morning, noon, and happy hour, to the bar downtown, across from the stadium, with the "Free Beer Tomorrow" sign in its window.

She never smelled the pungence of dumpsters, the sweet vapors of maryjane, nor tasted the fecal essence of Limburger. He'd become a regular raging drunk ever since McClarty's Bar posted its come-on.

She and he, despite minor deficiencies, prevailed in their unlikely union precisely because she couldn't detect his bibulous reek, his pugnacious B.O., hellacious halitosis, the tobacco smoke that corroded his shirts and pants, and he rarely had to look at her clothespinned nose, for being out of the house except to sleep it off, dreaming that his next visit to McClarty's would yield a veritable gusher of free beer.

Friends opined that theirs was indeed *the* perfect marriage.

No More Ants

The ants began manifesting their infestation at noon. By 2:30, they'd become ubiquitous — a colossal army of nasty invading insects swarming our kitchen sink and countertops, threatening our sanctum sanctorum with devastation.

We pretended that their presence wasn't obnoxious, rather an act of nature, like a cicada cycle erupting expectedly, every seventeen years or so, or maybe a consequence of our cleaning lady's vacation.

There they were, like legions of Nazi soldiers parading before the Reichstag, doing a jackbooted, goose-stepping victory march, crawling all over our cutlery set, our toaster, our Krups coffee maker.

Those ants kept coming, bumming us out. We wondered if we'd survive their onslaught or be carried away, down their trail, be eaten. As fast as we'd squash a squad, a hundred more would materialize.

Then my frantic wife ran to the utility closet, home to dozens of spray repellants, poisons, toxic cleaners, polishes, and the like, from which she grabbed a package of Terro Ant Killer. Systematically, in strategic locations, she laid down little cardboard patches, then poured the honeylike solution onto each.

Within minutes, hoards of the pismires converged on the liquid baits, trampling each other for a taste of ecstasy. We watched as they ate and rejoined the trail. Miraculously, in half an hour, all the thousands had retreated into the woodwork.

What a relief! No more ants — I mean none . . . that is, until we got into bed, naked, panting.

Christmas Visitation

This year, the final one of the millennium, Christmas just isn't in his emotional vocabulary, nor is his mind's generous thesaurus open to caroling relevant synonyms that might suffice in his time of dire depression. Even his trusty ency- clopedia, which does offer Chanukah, Ramadan, and Kwanzaa as far-fetched (to him) variations on the holiday, fails to satisfy his psyche's gasping appetite for a substitute, some cause for celebration, any reason to be festive during this dead-end season, when the very idea of buying gifts for anyone, himself included, all but immobilizes him.

For three weeks now, since Thanksgiving, he's drowsed in his apartment, like a torpid bear in its hibernal cave. He's not certain that the crass commercialism of Christ's birth is necessarily at the heart of his crisis or that his desperation derives from spiritual desolation.

After all, the etiology of his malaise might be explained away as "chemical deficiencies," a treatable imbalance of seratonin, dopamine, noradrenaline, in his brain's misfiring neurotransmitters. All he knows is that holing up in his two- room rental, unable to eat, watch TV, read (he hasn't show- ered or moved his bowels in twenty-three days), has brought on bloating in his abdomen, caused his neck, fingers, and toes to swell and turn yellow, his nose, ears, eyes, mouth, penis, and anus to bleed.

Swaddled in his putrescent shroud-sheets, he dreams that his hovel is the Church of the Holy Sepulcher and he's Jesus seeking eternal peace.

A-Pack-o'-Lips Now

This humpin' day mornin' over to Redbird's, them mackerel snappers's got a major heads o' steam up, sure's hell to beat a band of angels, what with them raggin' on that fat bastard (John or Jack the John-off or John the Jack-off — makes no differents whatsonever to me) about him bein' a combonation o' bein' fat 'n sick both to the same times and him tryin' without no luck to defense hisself, sayin' this is his onced-to-year cold, and him hackin' 'n wheezin' 'n snortlin' 'n blowin' his snout off into snot-rag after snot-rag, which means he keeps askin' all them other six snot-bags for their nakkins, which adds up to enough paper to print this mornin's addition of *USA's Today*, and then, onced they see they ain't gonna get too damn far baitin' his ass about his cold, even if they is secretly pissed he done brung it — that cold o' his — to the table, they take another aim, this time catchin' him in a more undefenseless mode, that havin' to do with him bein' fatter'n even *I* ever even seen him before.

"I'll lose these fourteen new pounds, boys, just as soon as we clear New Year's."

"Yeah, that's assuming we don't get stuck at the stroke of midnight, Friday night, and land back in 1901, driving a horseless carriage and having to load all the lamps with coal oil."

"Jesus, Sid! What kind of shit are you shoveling, this morning?"

"I'm serious. This Y2K isn't something to treat lightly."

"Well, I, for one, have all the confidence in this great country of ours to keep us out of any major problems."

"John, you mean you haven't been stocking up on water and C rations and two sides of beef to get you and Gladys through, from Friday night to Saturday morning?"

"From the looks of it, John doesn't need to do any stocking up."

"Not nice, Sid. Not nice."

"I mean, those three Belgian waffles you just downed ought to tide you over for at least a week."

"Boys, there's a scientific reason why I've been eating more than normal. It's a scientific fact that you've got to feed a cold and starve a fever."

"You sure it isn't feed a fever and starve a cold? That's what my grandmother-in-law used to say."

"Howard, I know that you can starve a fever, strange as it may seem, by eating so much you distract the cold from its mission."

"In that case, John, you should be cold- and fever-free for the next millennium."

"And fuck you too, Sid!"

So I'm listenin' to all this ignint shit, which I know them snappers feeds on, 'cause it's so easy to get that fat fartbag's Bill E. goat. But what a asshole o' him to think his fellow altered boys is gonna buy that starve-yourselfs-to-kill-a-cold's-fever shit. Anyone knows only way to nip a cold bud (and that don't mean no Bud Light, neither) in its tracks is to not contrack it in the first, second, and/nor third places neither, which I do by takin' a daily multiplied vitalman every day and a absorbic acid, along with two other vitalmans that's guaranteed to keep a guy's python from wiltin' on a cold day, sufferin' from fallin' to sleep on 'n off the jobs, if you catch the wrigglin' drift o' my trouser worm's draft.

Anyways, them loudmouths is runnin' their normal ski slope o' stupid stuff, like, for instants, how pissed they is as a table of one in unisal agreements on the lousy choice of EPNS choosin' their sportin' figure o' the millennial.

"Bud, what did you think about ESPN choosing Michael Jordan as Athlete of the Century?"

"What a crock of crap that is!"

"You bet. How they could've passed over giving it to Babe Ruth is beyond me. He made baseball what it is today."

"It's not beyond me. In fact, it's pretty goddamn obvious."

"And predictable, too."

"You bet, John. Who do you think pays to keep ESPN on the air? It isn't baseball, that's for sure. Since the strike, if it weren't for Mark McGwire, nobody'd even go to the games."

"Yeah, the NBA is their bread and butter."

"OK. I grant you Michael Jordan's a great athlete, a great American and a great Christian, too, but . . ."

And at that impregnable pausational, it ain't only obvial to them snappers from the House of the Holy Rollin' Pope Pile the 69th, built in 1492, but to me as well, too. I mean, even a dumb 'n deft-mutable, three-legged, tailless, Heinz 69 malomutt couldn't miss what was comin' if you even only knew them assholes from a distants the lengths 'n breaths o' the French Channel between Germania 'n London. I mean, even God Hisself would have to know what was comin' next.

"But . . ."

And the whole table goes into a kind o' weird disappearin', hush-hush act by followin' their own eyelids down over their own eyes, which, it's obvial, is somehow reinvokin' the ostrick gimmick, where a guy can bury hisselfs in the sands o' time, up to his heads 'n down to his assholes, and know no one else is gonna see what he's thinkin' or just done axeldently said by mistake.

"But he's a great *nigger*, too! And that's the point."

But maybe it's not. Face it, even if they done chose Hank Heron over the Sulfur of Swat, he couldn'ta kept EPSN in war bucks, since people hate baseball.

"You know what's really sick? Those 'dot-com' bowls. It's like without the blacks and technology companies, all sports today would come to a screeching halt."

"Did you see where, tomorrow, they're going to be running twenty-four hours of Tiger Woods on one of the TV channels?"

"Yeah, on ESPN, I think."

"Sid, you gonna be watching?"

"Not me. I'm strictly a Michael Jordan fan."

So I'm just sittin' here, tryin' to catch my breaths so's I can down my ham-steak-'n-chicken-stripped-eggs omlit (it's a special Cookie 'n me's worked up over the last few years or so, whenever he's got some good leftovers left over from night before; don't matter to me none what he throws into them eggs omlit, so long's it ain't toxical; personably, I love when he gets a turnup truckload o' mushedrooms and throws 'em into the witch's brewsky for good measurements; I'm always hopin' that, one day, we'll get some o' them real wild ones — the magicianal mystery tour kind, that kinda keep you on the tits o' your toes, if you catch the drift o' my draft), and I'm dreadin' goin' into work, even though we got Friday off for Nude Year's Eve (wonder if they named this holiday after Atom's Eve), which me 'n every other stiff over to Saturn 69's assemblage plant over to Fenton's gonna be needin' to recupinate from the K-Y2 bug that's been infectin' everything it sees, everything that moves, everything that's ever been buried or dead for the last hunnerd years, more nor less, recupinate as well from havin' overdid the Nude Year's celebatin', that I guarangoddamnteeya everyone 'n his mother's great-grandparents-in-laws from Bozzoslobovia 'n Madagascan 'n Sizzley's gonna be doin' to blow out the old and blow in the new millennial in fine formats.

"Sid, are you feeding a fever or starving a cold — or both?"

"Guys, I guess I'm probably just a little bit rattled over this whole Y2K thing. You know, it is possible that what they're saying about complete meltdown of the planet could happen."

"Come on, pal. Clinton says the government's fully compliant, and so is he — with Monica Lewinsky!"

"Stop screwing around! You guys can chalk this off if you want, but Mabel and I think this could be the real Apocalypse at hand, Revelation right on our front porch —

you know, what St. John saw: the Four Horsemen, the beast, with 666 on its head, the seven seals, and the seven bowls — the end of the world."

"Sid, I didn't realize you were such a good Catholic."

"John, it doesn't have anything to do with me being Catholic. The whole world runs on computers, and if just one computer fucks up at 12:01, you'll see an entire chain reaction of dominoes that takes the whole world down with it."

"Holy shit, Sid! Give it a rest, my man. We're going to be all right."

"Yeah, St. Sid. The world's going to survive the Apocalypse."

"And even if it doesn't, Sid, we'll still be here at Redbird's, all together, come Monday morning, even if it is in Heaven — or Hell!"

"And fuck you too, John!"

Jeezus! I, for a pack of one, is sicker'n shit in a portal-potty in a die-a-real ward, hearin' about this damn computer-itch-glitch shit. I can't finger out why, if them Silicone Valley o' the Dead Geeks is so fuckin' ingenieal, how come they couldn't finger out how to make them maimed-frame CP's o' theirs go from 1999 to 2000 instead o' flippin' all the way back to when them dinosours 'n anfibrians swum the earths 'n the skies, when God was just beginnin' to begin his "in the beginnin'" shit, if you catch the drift o' my Book o' Genitals draft. I mean, give me a fuckin' break! How a few techno-geek freaks, holed up inside their CP's, could take a whole whirl, a whole universal, hostages, so to speaks, is beyond 'n beneath me boths. Granite, I ain't much with computers myselfs, but I ain't against progressed neither. Still 'n yet, how them little bastards (and this time, they ain't even them Nips from Japland) could get all us humans scared so shitless o' the 12:01 that's comin' two days from tonight is a mystery over two to me, myselfs, 'n a I for a I.

I mean, give me a fuckin' break! That a ban o' rent-agade computer whizzers could bring a-pack-o'-lips to the whole planet, turn it into one o' them Germanial cream-matin' machines, where they baked 'n barbecued them Jewical kikes from Polakland 'n Ruskia 'n the Bozzo-slobovians from Hungry 'n Grease 'n Turkey durin' the war between the states o' Japland 'n Nitaly 'n Germania itself . . . bring the whole planet down around itselfs, don't make no sense to no one's logicals, 'specially not even mine.

That shit don't scare me none. Fack is, me 'n my buddies thinks it's all been so blowed out o' proportionals, Earth as it's known to Earthlinks may never come back down to Earth. I, as a party o' one for the party o' the Nude Year's Eve, which my good buddy Brotherton's agreed to hold against his will 'n over his wive's uneagerness to particilpate unless the rest o' us roughs agree to contribulate to all the party fixin's 'n feed bags . . . I, for one 'n for all, damn well know where *I'll* be between 12:00 'n 12:01, come Friday night comin'. I'll be havin' "a-pack-o'-lips" o' my own — my old lady's labialar lips, that is! Me 'n her's gonna be divin' in our bed o' oysters 'n clams (my Rocky Mountain oysters 'n her bearded clams, that is!), where, *come* what may (other than me 'n the missus comin' maybe ten times over 'n under!), no K-Y2 viral's gonna get a leg up on me 'n my old lady, guarangoddamnteeya.

Fell Out of Bed

The light-rail commuter trains, ZipLink, ran alongside the highway, for five miles, from their downtown terminal, then abruptly veered northwesterly, for two blocks, before running through the bedroom of his condo, under the Civil Courts Building — their final stop, where they disgorged passengers three times an hour.

Around-the-clock ZipLink service, the city's crown jewel, its chief mover and shaker, was a prime nuisance to residents along its routes; to mayoral and aldermanic bureaucrats, whose jobs were tied to its civic progress, it was an in-godsends-we-trust boondoggle in disguise. Regardless, it was a minor gridlock mitigator.

For the good of his fellow citizens, the fellow through whose bedroom the electric trains ran, every twenty minutes, with Nazi efficiency, never raised an eyebrow, a concern, a voice. In truth, he slept even more soundly (in the buff) for them; after all, their roaring was top-notch insulation material, with an R-440 rating, just like his snoring.

It ennobled him, knowing his digs were of some crucial use to the betterment of mankind. No regular riders, commuting from inner-city ghettos, to the courts complex, ever brought suit against his indecent exposure, viewable when he slumbered, between 10 p.m. and 5 a.m. Such were the unspoken protocols of eminent domain.

This arrangement had been in place a decade, during which the compliant condo owner and the Zip-State Development Corporation, managers of record for the labyrinthine light-rail system, rocked no boats, left well enough alone.

And none of his neighbors in the subterranean condo ever doubted that the cacophony was more than just his snoring, until one evening, that is, just days after he passed away, when a maintenance lady, doing routine inspection of the tentacular HVAC ducts, discovered him on the floor, supine, spread-eagle, his left hand still grasping the third rail of the tracks laid through the middle of his bedroom, his flesh black as a charred ballpark hotdog.

Can't Get Them Out of His Head

Three or four or five tunes blast his psyche to smithereens, with their intertwining of nauseating refrains that tie the remains of his brain's Möbius strips into macramé basket-hangers, orb and funnel spider webs, hummingbird nests, dangling, by threads, from the edges of a wind tunnel running in reverse, at full speed, threatening to suck him, bodily, into oblivion, as millions of dissociated notes seeking the open mouths of low-flying angels or black holes they might fill with their immemorial cacophonies — debris from "We're Off to See the Wizard," "Amazing Grace," "Swing Low, Sweet Chariot," "Camptown Races," and "Ding Dong! The Witch Is Dead!"

"De Camptown ladies sing dis song,
Ding dong, ding dong!
De Camptown racist two miles long,
The Wicked Witch is dead!
I looked over Jordan, and what did I see,
Comin' for to carry me home?
A band of angels on a bobtail nag
Runnin' all night and all day.
Amazing grace, how sweet the sound,
That saved a witch like me.
I once was lost on the Yellow Brick Road,
But now I'm blind, can't see.
Doo-da! The Witch is dead! Which old Witch?
The bobtail wretch!
Doo-da! The Wicked Witch is grace, because,
Because, because, because, because, because . . ."

No matter how many ibuprofens he pops, he can't eradicate these fractured echoes. They churn in his cement-mixer mind. If only he could find a landfill, quarry, or construction site for a new dam, into which he could pour this horrific stuff, he might relieve the pain shredding his head, reconcile his differences with these song-demons, come to some amicable agreement by which he could recover from his blindness, see God, be carried in a chariot, pulled by a band of angels (Camptown ladies, really — black ones, at that), around a racetrack two miles long (a yellow-brick road, really), leading from Emerald City, past the dissolved witch, home again, to the Land of Peace and Quiet.

What's Up?

This morning — Friday, thank God! — the crew at the local restaurant resembles an extended family of chimpanzees or mandrills or gorillas or spider monkeys congregating in the lush green basin of a rain forest — Cameroon- or Gabon- or Congo-on-the-Mississippi.

Why I see primates other than Homo sapiens baffles my imagination. Could it be contempt, indignation, irascibility? Perhaps I'm harboring some deep dissatisfaction with mankind or disenchantment with the planet — misanthropy manifesting itself in late middle-age.

I'm no anthropologist, sociologist, or psychologist, no Ph.D. in Western civilization, with an emphasis on the human condition, its follies, foibles, noble deeds, and grandeur, no rabbi or priest or veterinarian either, certainly not a good judge of character.

So why the shift in perspective? What's so different about *this* Friday morning? Should I be worried for my existence? Is it significant that my waitress just brought me a breakfast consisting of a sprig of leafy twigs, five unpeeled bananas, and a bowl of termites?

Present Shock

These days, he can barely keep up with change. Technology dizzies his brain. Just contemplating how e-mail works boggles his meager imagination. (Then again, he's never comprehended radio or TV, either.) Himself, he still relies on his trusty mailman, who delivers, rain or shine, snow, sleet, hail, tornado, fallout, dogs. Even the way athletes in every sport shatter old records as a matter of daily course tells a similar story: revolutionary designs and materials for equipment — cutting-edge racquets, clubs, bats, shoes, tracks.

He's amazed by the multitudes who claim to be afraid of the Y2K bugaboo, who are installing solar panels in their houses, stocking up on generators, hand-cranked radios, glorified C rations — all in the name of survival.

He still prefers the privacy of his home or the security of Superman's favorite changing room — the telephone booth, with its folding door — to make his business and pleasure calls, not *in medias res* at a restaurant, ballpark, or men's room.

He has no quarrel with Mark McGwire's feats, but somehow, he still admires the Babe for having fueled his miracles with wieners and beer, not steroids and weight training.

And when the new millennium unfurls, the only thing on earth he'll be worrying about is whether he'll be left in the dark.

First Feasts
o' the Nude Year's First Holy Day

Redbird's is dead on its feets, this first Monday mornin' o' the Nude Year's, for more reasons'n three. Not only is everyone hung under 'n out to dry, but they're sicker'n a whole flock o' possums rottin' in the middle o' Highway 44, which leaves me with a Mexical standstill between me 'n them mackerel snappers, 'cause without me nor them, this place'd be deader'n eighteen doornails in one o' them tires o' Pope Pile's Popalmobile. And third, who ain't either sicker'n shit nor hung under 'n out must be bit by the K-Y2 bug spell, believin' in that a-pack-o'-lips shit, even though none o' them bugs bit nothing but the dirts, them end-o'-the-whirl geek-freaks afraid to come outten their houses for fears o' catchin' a glitch in the dick or the ass. Truth is, I ain't never seen this joint so empty o' mornin' stiffs.

Then again, about half that snapper table o' five stiffs is hackin' 'n snortlin' like a plague o' them flem-flue bugs. They mine as well not be here neither for contracktin' some kind o' bug or others, and me, by mistakes, only two tables away for not payin' attentions to where they parked their squatter's rights when they done coughed 'n hacked their ways in after I done already sat.

"Sid, sounds like you've really got a bad one."

"Hell. Would you believe I've lost fourteen pounds in a week?"

"I don't see how that's possible. You couldn't weigh more than 150 normally."

"I'm down to 134."

"Then what are you doing out?"

"Howard, I can't live without your company."

"John, maybe you gave Sid your cold."

"Yeah, but I got screwed — he lost the fourteen pounds I gained over Christmas."

"Yeah, and all you did was feed your cold and fever so well that they decided to hang around till next Christmas, right?"

"Bud, give it a rest. Truth is, I weighed more when I was born than Sid weighs now."

"I bet you *were* a bumper-crop baby, John!"

"Good, Howard."

And all I can do is sit here wishin' I was halfway acrost the city 'stead o' two tables away from them typhoidal Peter's Paul 'n Marys. All I need's a whopper of a flem-flue bug to bring me down! Seems like everybody's got the bug, even if it ain't the one that was supposed to come.

And you talk about bummers. Me 'n the old lady ended up havin' to get a last-minute sittin' over to Stompanato's, when Brotherton's wifes called at the eleventh-and-a-half hour, about 4:30, sayin' he was out 'n down for the count Dracula with the chills 'n fever 'n stuff, and could they take a rain checks on the Nude Year's Eve potsluck for next year, which I knew suited Brotherton's old lady to a T for two, 'cause she wasn't too worked up about havin' the two-do at her house noways, for all the aftershocks we roughs make with our horsin' arounds, if you catch the aroma o' my stablehand's draft.

So after tyin' on a major feast bag over to Stompanato's, the missus 'n me ended up Friday night tubin' out, like I give a shit over forty-two about what a bunch of yahoos in Timed Squares is doin' to celebate, all frothin' at the mouths just 'cause one gigantic testickle's gonna fall exackly at the drops o' midnight 'n anchor in the Nude Year's. I mean, give me some slack, cut me a fuckin' break. And imagine, all them peoples congrelgatin', at least five million of 'em accordian to the TV, and not even a single portal-potty in sight — no wonder all them faces was jumpin' up 'n down like they had a bug up their asses. Fack o' the matter was, here you got over five million human people all drunk up to their eyeballs, only their eyeballs ain't yellow for havin' to take one gigantic leak in unisal but brown from you know what — like, in truths, what you really had goin' there in Timed Squares was Manshattan's Great Nude Year's Eve Brownout. Good thing midnight got there on time, so's everybody could get back to their own johns 'n stop up the whole city's sewage system with one massive, big-ass flush.

I mean, not too damn excitin' for the year 2000. But I gotta emit that me 'n my helpmeat made the breast of it, if you acquire the drift o' my Kernel Lingus's finger-lickin'-good chickens. I mean, we did our very breast to have a ball of our own, come what may nor might, even if it was my balls that kept fallin' hourly on the hour and twiced on the strokin's o' midnight. And another good thing about havin' to spend Nude Year's to home was that I wasn't stuck in the middle o' no five million freaks all tryin' to keep from pissin' 'n shittin' up the planet 'n their selfs as well, 'cause every eighteen minutes on the hour or so, whenever one o' them brewskies would send my fuel gauge up over full, all I had to do was say, "Be right back, hon, don't go nowheres — gotta water my horse or, more to the point, my unihorn," and go into the john just off the rump room, where we was hangin' out 'n up to dry.

"Boys, whatever happened to the Feast of First Holy Day?"

"What do you mean, John?"

"Well, it usually happens on the first day of the New Year."

"Yeah, so what's the problem?"

"The first fell on Saturday."

"So?"

"I didn't think it ever happened on a weekend."

"What difference does that make?"

"Sid, how would you know?"

"Because I went to Mass and took Communion Saturday . . . and Sunday."

"Sid, you really are a good Catholic."

"Boys, didn't they used to call First Holy Day 'The Feast of Circumcision'?"

"Yeah, they did. Then they changed it to 'The Feast of Mary,' and then they renamed it 'The Feast of the Holy Name,' because it was more politically correct."

"You'd think they could make up their minds in the Vatican and, while they're at it, assign the same day in the week each year to hold First Holy Day, regardless of when the first day of the new year falls."

"Jesus, Howard. You're beginning to sound more and more like Sid every day."

"Thanks for the compliment, John. It's not like you."

"I always get this way around the Feast of First Holy Day."

"Sure, John. We know. About once a year, providing you can figure out when it falls."

And me thinkin', the only good thing about this first day o' the Nude Year's was that it done come on a Saturday, which meant (and not necessarily in this order of importants), number one, that I didn't have to try to come back from the land o' the livin' deads to get my Nude Year's ass over to Fenton; number two, that I didn't have to risk contracktin' them bums' flem-flue bugs; and, number three, as well, that I could be to home with the missus on Saturday, all day, so's I couldn't not only get to catch up on all them collegial bowl games on TV — bitin' the hair of old Spuds, the Mackenzial dog that bit me Nude Year's Eve, with another couple o' six-packs of ol' Mr. Anthiser's Bush's best Bud Brewsky's Lights 'n Heavies — but start back up 'n continue again where we done left off Friday night at the strokes o' midnight, havin' our own Mary feast o' the circumcised pythons in the holy trinitarial names o' me, myselfs, 'n I times three to the third power over thirty-three, if you catch the drift o' my religional first feasts o' the Nude Year's draft.

Missing in Action

A Mekong Delta morning — every street and bare tree sweating, the air heavy with wetness — inundates his disposition. It could be light rain the radio predicted yesterday or remnants of a drunken blitz that split his vision, fried his brain to a crisp either in his dreams or earlier last evening, when he disappeared in a numinous monsoon (a recurring hallucination from his tour of duty in Vietnam, back in '69, '70, and '71) and was declared missing in action by his heart's Department of the Army.

No month is exempt from his memories of the jungle, that desperate claustrophobia interwoven with spiders, mosquitoes, snakes, sniper bullets shredding the air like bayonets, monkey screeches indistinguishable from cries of his buddies, as they lay dying from lead bites, shrapnel, disease, and fright, and always the nagging drizzle or torrential downpours lasting for days, weeks, thirty years now, drenching him in unabating terror, stalking him like the Vietcong, who would break his fingers and toes with mallets, carve out his private parts, ream his rectum with a red-hot poker.

Where he is, this morning of the perpetual wetness that turns trees to shivering bones, streets to arteries running cold under his skin, windows to eyes glazed over with winter's blinding mist, through which he stumbles and trudges, hacking at its impenetrable nets with vision's machete . . . where he's located, amidst morning's wetness, is anybody's guess but his. His wisdom is a catalyst for ambiguity.

All he suspects is that last night, he and his platoon were slogging through a rice paddy, when cross fire took them out, every last one of them — including him, in his alcoholic stupor.

Ozymandias Redux

I met a man from an antique land (it could easily have been Samothrace or Samarkand), grotesquely hirsute from fingertips to toes, who had five arms, eight legs, protruding from his potato-shaped trunk, and a triad of satyrs' faces suspended from the end of a retractable tail wound on a titanium reel anchored tightly in one of the six-inch-wide anuses inside his engorged, bright-pink cluster of seven buttocks.

Even more curious to my gentle sensibility were this creature's three penises — attached where his tongue should have been — flicking spasmodically, as if licking the air for scents of female genitalia, possibly just feeding on insects.

No stranger man in any stranger land did I meet (it could easily have been the manticore's lair) as I passed on my crusade to Canaan, in quest of the Holy Grail, which Joseph of Arimathaea may have buried in those inhospitable, lone, and level sands flowing, shifting, swirling over countless tells, where, once, in civilizations predating history, time and eternity dwelled side by side.

That deformed throwback, freak of nature, that beast, that stinking manimal, with his leering sneer of stony, cold command, standing at the crossroads of the Dead Sea and Nowhere, stopped me, begging directions — or a drink.

I, being in a hurry to fulfill my glorious destiny, paid him no heed.

Satan Plays Devil's Advocate

Where do you go, when there's no drawing board to go back to? And how do you continue hopscotching to the semicircle at the end, when you keep retreating to square one, without your lucky rock? How do you strategize starting from scratch, when you've led a charmed life, never had to wrangle with disaster, impoverishment, take stock of negligible accomplishments, be accountable for your selfish actions?

In truth, you haven't a clue what to do, now that the bottom has dropped out, the roof has fallen in, the moon has eclipsed the sun. You could run from your shadow if broad daylight weren't so obscure, erase the graffiti on your spirit's cave walls, using your piss for vinegar, if it didn't burn so painfully when you urinate, and the stalactites weren't throbbing with bats. You could crawl onto a highway and play possum.

Maybe you could lay low, take time to contemplate fate's estate, consider which options, if any, exist for you, now that your condition, as yet undiagnosed, has reached such dire straits. Up to your hips in alligators, you could pray for a deus ex machina to pluck you from your conscience's abyss at the eleventh hour, in a New York minute, at the last possible second, in the blink or flick of a cosmic eye or wrist.

But I'm not sure, if I were you, I'd be all that eager to take my advice. I've had my share of skeptics, defectors, heretics, who've thrown their lots in with mine, diced in the temple of lies, glad to be party to my schemes to extricate them from their tights, only to have them repent, renege on our gentleman's agreement, slink home to mom and dad — Dad especially. Best think twice! The last laugh's always mine!

How you got yourself out on this flimsy limb, Picassoed into such a corner, flew past the point of no return, on your

half-filled tank of cuckoo juice, got stranded between no-
man's-land and limbo, grasping for straw partners, crawling
on your belly, groping to locate an opening out of your
soul, on this darkest midlife night, can only be explained
as left-brain bad luck. Nobody in his right mind could have
gotten this fucked up — not even me!

Total Freedom

These days of his post–senior citizenship, in the republic of late-age languishers, he finds it as easy to go as to stay. It's not that places are closer, transportation more efficient, quicker, cheaper, so much as that leaving is irresistible. Death makes it inviting, enticing, by not restricting admittance to its necropolises: oases, exotic isles, gardens, pleasure domes, Heaven. Those from all provinces, dominions, principalities, orders, genuses, species, and religious, ethnic, gender, and sexual predilections are welcome anytime, night or day. And it offers a variety of cut-rate packages, guaranteed to fit everybody's budget, from wards of the welfare state to Bill Gates.

But the greatest incentive to depart with whatever frequency chance or fancy allows is that when he does, he takes his entire earthly estate with him. He has nothing that if stolen or destroyed (by vandals or acts of God irrelevant) could affect his utter nothingness, since he rents the implements of his existence by the hour. He doesn't even own his clothes, false teeth, prosthetic hips, pacemaker, colostomy bag; his sofa, bed, toilet, stove, medicine, and moods are part of a lease-to-own program.

What most suits his circumstances, these days, is that even his senses don't know when he takes leave. The last time he had such total freedom was before birth, ninety years ago.

A Minkey in the Wrenchworks

You'da thought, sure as flamin' dogshit in a dog bag over to Dogtown, that them snappers woulda made it into Redbird's this Monday mornin', of all mornin's, since it's ol' Marlin Luther the Junior King's big day, today. I mean, them mackerel snappers don't hold down no steady jobs noways, don't even hold down no unsteady jobs neither, which'd make this a perfeck excuse for comin' in here to waste the whole mornin' chewin' the shit, shootin' the fat, and givin' the blacks a big in-your-faces up-your-assholes by comin' in to Redbird's to do their work, which consists o' stirrin' up the shit — and that ain't just dogshit neither but closer to elephump- 'n spermaziti whale- 'n dinosour- 'n dragonshit too, if you catch the whiff o' my driftin' drafts.

Only, on third 'n fifth thoughts, maybe I see the logics o' their unlogicality, them not comin' in today, on this holiday for some — me 'n Saturn No. 69 included in the celebatin'. Maybe it's their way o' bad-mouthin' blacks 'n nigs 'n jigaboos 'n Afurcan-a-Mericans 'n jungled bunnies, a way o' puttin' up a white-picket-fence line o' racial cards, or some such, their way o' sittin' in, so to speaks, by sittin' out. In fack, by not showin' up this mornin', you could say them unmoral dicktators o' the publics taste in ethicals, political uncorrections, 'n religional insurrections is doin' their own inconspiculous sit-out in honor o' the King o' Spades (which, I guess, is the best my line boss out to Saturn 69, Alferneeze, 'n his bunch o' minkeys can do, since them Cathlicks already done called dibs times 8.5 on the King o' Hearts, ol' Jesus P. Christ on two crutches o' crosses, He, Hisselfs, 'n Him).

Anyways, the real question in my mind o' minds is what in hell I'm doin' here, since not only Saturn 69 ain't open today but the roads is half empty and I'm still half full o' the good Bud brewsky I done downed during yesterday's whuppin' o' them Vikin's on the fox's TV nutwork, who done boated down the Missus Sloppy from Lake Minnesoda to play our St. Louis Cardinal Rams for the half-titles of our leagues (I can't never keep straight the NCF from the ALCU, NAPCP from the ACF 'n all their divisionals). All I do know is that one more win at the TWAT Dome, and our boys'll be goin' to play the Atlantas in the Stupor Bowl down to the Georgian Frontier, which is a unheard o' stunt, 'cause in the last thirty years I been tryin' to follow local hometown pigskinizations here in good ol' St. Louis, groin 'n hairy armpits o' the Hardland, we ain't never so much as had so much as a single star player, let alone a team anyone would even wanna forget, let alone remember longer'n it takes to forget 'em forever, certainly nobody like Martial Falcon, Bruce Isaac, five-hundred-pound Whorelando "the Refrigerators" Pacemaker, 'n Captain Kirk Warners.

Anyways, why I'm in Redbird's, 'stead o' sleepin' in, is fuckin' unpossomable to say, since I wouldn'ta even had to phone in sick to Alferneeze, my assemblage line boss, 'cause he ain't even there, since it's his holiday, and it'd look real bad if he showed up (even if they did open up the lines for us white guys who need the double time more than the sleep), like he don't have no respect for peoples o' colored; and 'cause I'm surprisin'ly unhung over 'n under 'n out, which means that I guess two six-packs weren't even enough to get the better 'n the best o' me, let alone the worst, yesterday; and 'cause I ain't even sick with them fuckin' flemflue bugs, which is goin' around St. Louis like a band o' fagnit gypsies tearin' through a dognut shop.

Anyways, I'm sittin' here in this half-empty eatery, wonderin' what I'm gonna do if I don't go home and sleep it off after I scarf down some grub, even if I ain't got nothin' to sleep off that I couldn't live with even if I did have to get into the plant today, sittin' here thinkin' how bodacious them Cardinal Rams was yesterday against them Lake Minnesoda Vikin's, thinkin' how it's a damn good thing that game was played yesterday and not today instead, 'cause then you'd have that whole damn indoors TWAT Dome, with its fake grass 'n 150,000 seats with all their noise, and only about eight players on both teams combined, standin' down there on the fake grass, tryin' to get up a white minority of a black majority, like maybe four to five honkies on one team, maybe three lily-white guys on the other team, not enough combined to make up a full team on one team, and a crowd of 150,000 screamin' uncolored fantasticals cheerin' for their team, 149,969 of 'em anyways, since them seats was runnin' somewheres in the neighborhoods o' five hunnerd dollars nor less per seat, which thus 'n therefore unincluded about ninety-nine 'n ninety-nine tenths of a percent o' the black copulation o' the entire city ghetto — thirty-one seats, more less than more — cheerin' for a team o' no players on one side o' the ball 'n only seven nor eight whities down in their stances 'n crotches on the other, tryin' to finger out how to run plays against a black no-show phantom team and make it look like a real game's happenin' anyways, so's that the TWAT Dome, where Pope Pontius Pile the 69th, from the Fattycan in Polandia, kissed Mike McGwire's finger while Big Mike washed his toes, won't be shamed outten all existence for bein' called big-gutted 'n undiscriminal 'n nonracially disorientated, if you acquire the drift o' my shifty draft.

I mean, if they'da played this play-off-'n-on today, you'd have about a half o' dozen white guys show up 'n about two hunnerd black players nowheres to be found, since they'd be doin' a sit-out to protest holdin' the game on Marlin Luther the Junior King's day o' days, claimin' they was bein' undiscriminated against. And, worst, what if one day they, our Senatobials 'n Sales Reps, them unofficially selected members of our governin' body parts, get forced into pickin' a second nig to celebate, 'cause they had to look like they was doin' somethin' to keep their jobs by equalin' out the playin' field, evenin' it up 'n down — separated but racial-card equality o' the fittest — you know, findin' another jig, so's they could have a pair to match our ol' Dishonest Abe 'n Boy George, the third first father of our cuntry . . . and what if that guy had to be another nig, like Louie Furrycan or that Reveral Michael Jesse Jackson, with the Rainbow's Correlicktion, or Mark "The Ear Rapist" Tyson . . . hopefully, at least them Senatobials 'n Sales Reps in the three houses o' Congrass will have the good common horse senses to hold his holiday on a Tuesday, *not* a Monday, so long's it don't inflict with the regular pigskin season nor during the playoffs. If they bungled that, they'd fuck up the entire game o' football in a Merica as we know 'n love it today — imagine no *Monday Night's Football* for a night!

But thank God there ain't two infamous Afurcan-a-Mericans — that is, unless you exclude Okra Windfree 'n Alferneeze "Geez, Can't See Ma Knees" Johnson — 'cause then, with two nigaboos, there'd be too much pressure on Mr. Anthiser's Bush to shut down his brew plant over to Pestalousy 'n Broadways for the day, and that, guarangoddamnteeya, would really throw a minkey — a eightthousand-pound, lowlife silverblack gorilla — into the wrenchworks.

The Crime

In last night's dream, he's fleeing ghosts with gas cans. He can't tell whether they're wearing white sheets or glowing, but he knows they're on a tear and that their dogs are foaming at the mouth, drooling on his forehead and neck — or is it beads of bloody sweat?

Why he's being assailed, he has no clue, unless it has to do with a crime he might have committed earlier, in the labyrinth of this hallucination, which yet consumes him in guilt: the murder of his wife and two children, which makes his a blatant case of mistaken identity, since he's never been married.

Strange lights that might be angels or meteors hover high above a mountain on fire, to whose peak he's climbed, over nanoseconds, minutes, hours, lifetimes (time is a spider's web flapping in a hurricane, its bridge lines connected to the horns of forty rhinos chasing him from sleep, into waking).

Suddenly, he's a human torch, whose flame gives off light so bright its radiance extinguishes the mountain's conflagration, turns it into a drizzle of lush-green rain forest swarming with rhinos, spiders, dogs, specters — yesterday's dross forming a bridge to this morning, where he awaits sentencing for his crime.

Roy Lichtenstein's Ladies

So I have the whole afternoon to kill, just the two of us, me and Jefferson, my eleven-month-old son — day care closed for the three-day weekend — and I decide to take us to the National Gallery to get a touch of culture for free, and they had a Roy Lichtenstein exhibition, which I really liked, pretty much — all those blown-up comic-book pages, in frames, showing half-dressed ladies trying to keep from being raped, et cetera, thugs and good guys slugging it out, "POW!"s and "ZAP!"s and "WOW!"s floating between balloons rising from their mouths.

And I'm enjoying this art a lot, because the black lines, red, yellow, and blue dots, are all working to soothe my eyes, not excite them, even with all the action happening, and all of a sudden, this security guard comes up to me, sitting on a bench, resting (Jefferson's like a sack of potatoes after you carry him for ten or twenty minutes), using the occasion as an excuse to breast-feed my son, with the hopes that this'll keep him from crying, disturbing the others come to see the art, and just as nasty as you please, like *I'm* the sack of potatoes or a bag lady, the guard says to me, "Ma'am, no eating or drinking."

And I look up, kind of startled, you know, because I'm just sitting there, feeding my baby, not bothering anyone in the place, and I say, "I'm begging your pardon," and he repeats his warning, and I say, "But I'm not eating or drinking, though I wouldn't mind a little water," and he says, "Don't get smart with me, lady. I can have you removed." And I say, "What's your beef, mister?" and he says, "You're ruining the viewing pleasure of gallery patrons. Please leave now." And I go silent, choke up, start to cry, pull my son off the tit, reclasp my nursing bra.

By this time, there must be ten of them, all dressed in security-guard uniforms, gathered around Jefferson and me and this guy, making such a fuss, the whole museum seems to stop. It's like me and my son are in a frame, hung on the wall, for all to study our dots, all our "POW!"s and "WOW!"s and "ZAP!"s and "WHAM!"s, and I can't believe this is happening to me.

Then this official man in a blue suit scatters the whole crew and apologizes to me, like none of this ever happened and never should have, like he hopes I'll accept his apologies, forget it all, and come back, whenever I want, for a "private tour" — like I'd ever step foot in that place again.

I'd Walk a Mile for a Camel

Symbols, ironies, nuances, ambiguities, paradoxes, metaphors, subtleties of dialogue, hyperboles, incongruities, absurdities, synecdoches, modestly satirical proposals, bons mots, absurdities à la Jason Compson and Joseph K.: a menu of *basse cuisine* from which writers bereft of true imagination select their trifling truffles, frail snails, fake crabmeat (beggar's caviar), hog brains (poor man's beef Wellington), Ben & Jerry's Cherry Garcia ice cream, Jell-O instant pudding, Fruit Loops, Nilla Wafers, masquerading as soufflés, bananas Fosters, crème brûlées.

Whoa! Hey, just hold your Percherons, your Tarpans, your Clydesdales, your goose-stepping Lipizzaners, your Przewalski's horses. Whoa! Whoa, Nellie! Let's rein it in, big time, Bob (it's gettin' kinda chilly out here! Frost's on the plump pumpkins, all right!), 'cause whose snowy woods these are, I think I know, though they're infested with Gestapo agents, Sonderkommandos, and Einsatzgruppen, on loan from Warner Bros. Studios, to film yet one more Looney Tunes docudrama on the Holocaust, one more *Schindler's List* (directed by Mel Brooks), to prove to history's wannabe revisionists that the Shoah was the ultimate show-and-tell pietà.

Whoa, kemosabe, Madeline Kahn, Cleavon Little! How in blazing saddles did we get here, anyway, stranded so far from Yoknapatawpha, where logic is Benjy Compson and Ike Snopes and home is an untranslatable hieroglyph for death? Whoa, Mr. Ed! A horse may be a horse may be a horse, of course, but that don't necessarily equate you with Ed Sullivan introducing his "really big shoe," if you catch the pas de deux of my verbal dressage. I mean, not everything depends on red wheelbarrows, loaded with Jew corpses, beside Topf & Sons ovens, painted white with electrified-barbed-wire chickens.

Oh, if only W. C. Williams had met W. C. Fields and W. C. Handy in the w.c. at Auschwitz-Birkenau-Buna, he might have changed his tune, written Wallace Stevens, T. S. Eliot, and Ezra Pound, clued bigotry's baddest bards in, to the Final Solution, one Jew-baiting generation early.

Ah, but where does all this leave us/me, who, at the tail end of the second millennium, are/is left to sweep up the leavings of equine? (That's "cakes," "pucky," "dung," "pats," "flops.") Old Bob Frost's little horse must think him queer, so full of shit that his really big shoes squeak — he's in dire need of being reshod.

Give Bartleby the last word: "I prefer camels; they're mild!"

Stertor Restertus

He unleashes a volley of short snores and an explosive sneeze that scares him out of sleep like a camper discovering a bear rifling his tent. Too suddenly, he's delivered himself to consciousness, sunlight slicing through the blinds, roiling fluids cresting in his flood-stage bladder. If he doesn't hurl his lumpy body to vertical within a matter of decisive seconds, he'll saturate his pajamas, drench the sheets of his Hide-A-Bed.

The parquet floor stabs his feet with splinters as he stumbles toward the toilet, down the corridor leading from the add-on porch, to which, five years ago, his wife of four decades exiled him, claiming his snoring sounded like a steam calliope or a herd of feeder cattle stampeding a salt lick, that it caused earthquakes to ravage Turkey, Egyptian mummies to break out of their wrappings, and frozen sperm to thaw and swim upsteam.

For five years, now, he's sought sleep as a refuge not from life but from the kvetching of his crotchety wife, Cassie, her nagging, carping, fault-finding, nitpicking about the clothes he wears, the utensils he selects to attack his food, her correcting of his attempts to carry on a conversation, express a mildly dissenting opinion, even his submissive compliances to her wishes (he's too polite to call them orders, commands, preferring to think euphemistically, optimistically — it takes fewer facial muscles to smile than to frown or scowl or retaliate).

And so, for five years, except for sojourns in the bathroom and kitchen, he's holed up on the porch, not left the house, rarely engaged Cassandra, and reveled in his freedom to snore his ass off, come what may — horses, beeves, mummies, sperm, Turkish earthquakes . . . his wife.

I Have a Dreams

"Boys, I had a dream."

"What kind of a dream, John? A wet dream?"

"Boys, I had a dreeeeam."

"I'll bite."

"I had a dream that a helicopter came down out of the sky and hovered over Janet Reno as she was giving her speech down at the Old Courthouse, yesterday, drowned her out, hung a Confederate flag from the pole, atop the dome, then flew off, right through the Arch, with her standing there, shaking in her boots."

"Literally."

"Sid, that's not a nice thing to say about your attorney general."

"I can't help it that she's got Alzheimer's."

"It's Parkinson's, Sid."

I knew them irreveral bastards couldn't keep their irreveral mitts off that Marlin Luther the Junior King's Day. They always gotta run whatever's in the air into the ground, good thing or otherwides. And me wonderin' how assholes like them coulda been brought up in a pinocchial school, where they shoulda learned how to treat all peoples o' color 'n noncolor with the same disrespect they reserve, for havin' been taught by nones in penguin suits 'n popes in white robes, and them trained to be altered boys kneelin' 'n lightin' candles every two seconds on top o' that, or so I been told. I mean, you can almost expect roughs like me 'n myselfs to have a on-occasional on-handed remark nor three for colored peoples o' colors 'n Jews 'n alien foreigners 'n neon-Nazis 'n fagnits 'n immigrunts from Sizzley, where they grow mafias in with their olives 'n regatta headcheese 'n wine grapes 'n spaghettis o' all shapes 'n colors 'n stripes 'n shades 'n lengths 'n breaths, which they ship to a Merica in biscuit 'n olive-oil tins, plasdick bags, 'n in their bottles o' Gianti . . . can almost expect to get a on-colored-person- or dago- or Polack- or Jew-fagnit-commie-hippie-HVI-joke every onced to a while, 'cause roughs like me, myselfs, 'n I was sort o' left to our cuttin' up in school, them knowin' we was gonna gradulate one way or another or not as what they call blue-rings-around-the-collar stiffs. . . . I mean, somebody's gotta work beside by sides with the rest o' them melted pots, and for goddamned-to-hell sure it ain't gonna be them mackerel snappers, with their fancy religional edjewcations and their bein' born into a sure-thing life with gold 'n silver spoons 'n forks 'n carvin' knives shoved so far up their butts they look like they got peacock tail feathers when they take off their duds.

"Boys, can you believe South Carolina?"

"They've got a lot of guts, I'd say. It takes real balls to know you're going to make national TV and still fly a Confederate flag over your state capital."

"I'm surprised the blacks don't do a trillion-man march on those bigots."

"Sid, there aren't more than a few million blacks in the first place, and most of them are in the football playoffs or at home watching them."

"Howard, that doesn't sound like the Howard I know."

"All I'm saying is that the country needs somebody to bring all the racial stuff to a head again, so that we can feel guilty enough to cut them some more slack."

"And what better exposure than on MLK Day?"

"That's right. How else are we going to have affirmative action and the end of racial profiling shoved down our throats, if we don't show a bunch of blacks, with a smattering of white guys, protesting a Confederate flag fluttering in their faces above their state capital?"

"Controversy breeds progress, I always say."

"I've never heard you say that, John."

"Sid, put a sock in it."

"Listen, if Strom Thurmond wants to continue to vote

Confederate, not shoot until he sees the whites of their eyes, that's his business."

"That's true, Bud. The guy's about ninety-nine years old, which makes him almost a boy when the Civil War was still going."

"Not exactly, Sid. Then again, your math never was that hot."

"Hope you can at least figure out the tab — it's your turn, this morning."

"Boys, we're just damn lucky we live in such a liberal city. St. Louis is really very open and integrated and committed to the separation of church and state, state's rights, and the abolition of the welfare state."

"Holy shit, Bud. Maybe you should have been up on that podium with Janet Reno, yesterday."

"Yeah, I bet Bud could've brought Dred Scott and his wife back from the dead, with that shit."

And me knowin' you give any one o' them guys half a chance or less, they'll chew your cud to a pulp, be the first to claim executal privileges for keepin' nonundesirables outten their pinocchial monasteries 'n crapitals 'n such. As for me, I sorta think them guys from South Carolinia maybe shouldn'ta flew the flag so in-your-faces, shoulda maybe just kept doin' all their segregatin' behine closed doors, shoulda kept all them saber-rattler ghost-snakes in their water closets, if you catch the thrust o' my trouser-sword, my uniform's unicorn.

On the other hands, I ain't too damn sure that I unprove o' them blacks from the NAPCP protestin' like they might wanna climb all over the crapital down there and rip the flag clean off its pole, I mean, the pole clean outten the dome, the dome clean outten the crapital, the crapital clean outten the ground, the ground clean outten the Confederal States of a Merica. I mean, that don't look too damn good neither on TV, that 'n them threatenin' to boycat South Carolinia by stoppin' all its tourists at the borders and sendin' 'em back to home. I mean, I got a real problem with people gettin' uncivilized in publics, whether it's blacks nor whites nor pinks nor polka dots. Things like this shouldn't be done on TV for people like them Cathlicks here in Redbird's to be able to make fun of. I'd like to see what woulda happened if someone done flown the flags of Israbia or Nizrael from the tops o' the cathedral dome down to Lindell when Pope Pile the 69th done made his two-day crusade in his Popalmobile all the way from Tia-jew-wanna to good ol' St. Louis. Yeah, I'd like to see how many o' their tribe they'da rousted out to protest down Lindell.

"Boys, how about that game, Sunday? Was that something else?"

"Isn't it amazing how excited everybody is now? Just a year ago, everybody was putting ads in the paper to sell their PSL's for two hundred bucks apiece, seats they paid five thousand bucks for, for the privilege of renting by the year. And look now — they're as good as gold. A guy could get a liver transplant easier than a PSL."

"They were something, weren't they? But I've got to tell you, for my money, I had the best seat in the house."

"Where was that, John? Were you in the first row on the forty?"

"Howard, I was right in my rec room, in front of my fifty-inch Mitsubishi, and I could see everything, even the whites of their eyes. And I never missed a minute's worth of the action, for all the replays. Like I said, best seat in the house."

That fat-ass mighta had the best seat in the house, his house, but, guarangoddamnteeya, I had one o' the hunnerd best seats in Fubar's, along with my buddies, Bobbitt 'n Kowalski 'n Brotherton, and we saw all the action too, up close 'n personable, and I don't just mean the pigskin action neither, which, I gotta emit, was bodacious as hell, but the action from the special squad o' ponpond cheer-leaders they hired on for the day to keep us roughs satisfied through the entire game, knowin' we'd be puttin' an extra stress on the joint for the excitements of us havin' a playoff team for the first time in the two-hunnerd-year history o' the pigskin league, them cheerleaders all decked out in so little less than nothin' as to make the Hooters gals look like they was goin' in drag, even if Fubar's squad was made up of underaged high-school dropouts 'n runaways.

Oh, yeah, I mean to tell you, Sunday was some kind o' special Bud brewsky day for us guys. That fat-ass may've had his one fifty-inch Mizzou-bitchy slo-moin' 'n instant-replayin' 'n shit like that, but me 'n the guys had twenty-five o' them TVs goin' to beat all shit outten hell, so that every time Martial Falcon zigzagged the ball from Hell to High-water and every time Captain Kirk Warners threw the ball to his linemans, who, somehow, was legal 'n uneligible at the same times to catch his passes for TD's, what we saw was twenty-five TD's for every one that fat-ass saw, which, when you add in all them zillions o' replays added in for good measures, finally gave the St. Louis Cardinal Rams the biggest victory anyone's ever seen, comin' out to about 12,042 to 39. I mean, it was awesome.

All that ball aside (which I emit don't normally sound too damn much like me, myselfs, 'n me neither), all I gotta say is I also got a dreams. The dreams I got is that come to-morrow mornin', somehow them mackerel snappers at the Cathlick table grows fins 'n tails 'n slimy scales 'n bulgy eye-balls and somehow get helicoptered from Redbird's and dropped into the Missus Sloppy, where they can mix with all them other catfish 'n gars 'n electronic eels 'n whatnots and, somehow, ends up gettin' washed out into the Golf o' Mexico City, where Janet Rhino'll be on vacation with her shakes, deep-sea fishin' off the coasts o' Miami's Beach and, somehow, catches all o' them snappin' mackerels on her Lazy Ikes and throws 'em into the ice cooler for good. That's the dreams I got. And maybe, with a little luck, it'll pan out about as well as the dreams Marlin Luther the Junior King dreamed from his mountaintop motel in Memfins, Ten o' Seas.

The Hoarder

The third Saturday of each month is his Sunday-go-to-meeting treat to himself, his take-the-piggies-to-market day, his big chance to sell pigs' ears as silk purses, rob Peter's piggy bank to pay Paul's cookie jar, cast his cultured pearls before the piggies, give vent to his hunt-and-gather instincts for buying and selling, at the Belleville Flea Market, from his quadruple booth in the main building.

From 7 a.m. — rain, snow, or shine — when the dealers are permitted access to set up their wares, until 5 p.m., when the event's declared closed, he's a pterodactyl, swooping from stall to stall, collecting baubles, gewgaws, shards, artifacts, to feather his nest, steel his rookery against storms that would threaten his obsessiveness . . . when he can con his wife into manning the booth.

And to each potential purchaser of his stuff — his zirconia diamonds and rhinestones in the rough, his goods, oddities, stock in trade, relics, each a treasure from Solomon's chest — those who browse with bemused disinterest, those who gawk, dumbfounded, from the aisles, and those vision-ary few who appreciate true value, would never buy a pig in a poke, prefer the up-close-and-personal touch, and choose to enter into negotiations with him, dickering against his verbal expertise and infinitely quicker instinct for squeez-ing every cell of blood from their turnips without making them cry bloody murder . . . to each, he hands a xeroxed solicitation proclaiming, in unabashed handwritten detail, the infinite ambition of his acquisitiveness, that desire to corner the world market on things:

"I ACTIVELY OR PASSIVELY,
EITHER COLLECT, HOARD, OR BUY
THE FOLLOWING CATEGORIES:

1 Coins

2 Stamps

3 Tokens

4 Misc Type Tokens

5 Lucky Pennies

6 Post Cards

7 78 Records

8 33 Records

9 Play Boys Etc

10 Valentines

11 Greeting Cards

12 Stereograph Cards

13 European Beer Glasses

14 European Adv. Ashtrays

15 European Beer Coasters

16 Tie Clasps

17 Cuff Links

18 Bottle & Can Openers

19 Maps

20 Matches

21 Hot Sauces

22 Oranaments

23 Old Pictures

24 Casino Items

25 Cigar Band

26 Fishing

27 Shot Glasses

28 Old Books

29 16 mm Kids Films

30 Rulers

31 Trading Stamps

32 Key Chains

33 Marbles

34 War Ration Book

35 18 Scale Cars

36 Hotel Items

37 Demitas Cups

38 Mills

39 Old Magazines

40 Avon

40 Old Sachets

41 Old Documents

42 Old Paper Items

43 Some Tools

44 Cigar Boxes

45 Dice

46

47

48

49

50

I ALSO BUY ESTATES & CLOSE-OUTS
PLEASE CALL —
ZEV 'LEO' ZIMMERMAN
314-432-1771"

And so it is that the third Saturday of each month, he attends the Belleville Flea Market, to take in more, by far, than he jettisons, not caring in the slightest, really, whether he makes a profit or sustains a small loss on items that leave his booth, always hoping to go home with his coffers overflowing. Where he'll store his additional hoard is unimportant; what counts is the euphoria his things bring him.

Side Effects

Out of the clear blue, overnight, it seemed that follicle and dust mites became too much with us.

For years, we'd simply not considered the possibility that monsters might be invading our pores, sharing cavities on our scalp, in our eyesbrows and lashes, and, worse, not only devouring our skin cells but depositing their fecal matter, like crazy, all over our epidermises.

But just two months ago, a traveling salesman, in a picnic-tablecloth suit, sporting spats, handlebar mustache, and gold watch connected to a gold-link chain running, from his vest pocket, to a waistband hidden by at least a hundred pounds of flab, passed through our town, on a whirlwind selling spree, not three steps ahead of our scofflaw sheriff, whom he'd bribed for a percentage of his take.

He was hawking a "salvific anodyne" against mites. For five hours, like a fire-and-brimstone, "Sinners in the Hands of an Angry God" missionary, he fulminated, cajoled, taunted, and dared us to sample one tiny bottle of his elixir, his "tried-and-true, rhythm-method-proven" nostrum, to rid ourselves of the "pestiferous entomological irritants," those micro-scopic, spiderlike parasites — "Arachnids!" — that share our most intimate parts without our consent.

He was explicit, graphic, apocalyptic, hoping to frighten the whole rapt town with his histrionic allusions to Revela-tion's beast — "the 666 mites of Satan!" — repeating his dire litany: "Mites don't make right! God's might gets right with mites! One dose of Dr. Hiram B. Pinckley's Mite-Away will deliver you from the weevils of evil, the vermin that turn our wellsprings to Hell! Save your hide, if not your soul — that too!"

He had us spellbound, breathless, panting for a week's, month's, year's stock of that "guaranteed daredevil-mite exterminator." We townspeople fell to our knees and prayed that the "Right Reverend Highness of Mites" would not run short of demand's supply. We believed we were putting an end to a scourge we never knew existed, purging ourselves of those traffickers in the skin trade.

But within days, all of us were itching. Our various hairs were letting go their holds on our follicles, like autumn leaves. Then we began succumbing to hideous disorders: painfully inflamed pustules, bloody vomit, reeking green urine, diarrheal incontinence.

But Dr. Pinckley was nowhere to bear witness.

Our chemist, at the request of the coroner, tested a vial of Mite-Away and made his report: "Admixture of WD-40, 170-proof grain alcohol, Off!, Ovaltine, K-Y Jelly, and traces of d-Con, Nair, and Zyklon B."

Out of our population of 452, only ten were fortunate enough to survive. But those of us who did are indeed mite-free!

Cobra Man

It started rather innocuously, one night in college, when his fraternity brothers cajoled him into taking their binge-drunk dare, giving in to a trip to a nearby tattoo parlor, where the resident Picasso, in just under a painstaking, beer-numb hour, endowed his erect penis with an uncoiled serpent, whose menacing head was his glans.

It was a remarkable feat for artist and recipient alike, a tour de force, you might almost say, for its cleverness, its ability to delight spectators — the ultimate sexual titillation, turnon, to witness a hooded cobra, slumbering in its raffia basket (the guy's scrotum), slowly rise to its full striking height, of eight inches.

After that, he found himself the talk of the campus, the frat brother of choice whenever orgies were in progress in the "iniquity den." His reputation as a charmer grew legendary. He never spent two nights in a row with the same girl. Every female was curious and deserved to have her curiosity sated, or so went his service-oriented philosophy; after all, he was an equal-opportunity fuck.

Eventually, people quit calling him by his real name, Ted Apted, in favor of "Cobra Man," which they'd abbreviate to "Coby." His reputation as the "eighth wonder of the world" persisted for at least a year but then began to wane, as others copied his distinctive feature. The tattoo artist flourished with frequent requests for equally provocative hard-on artwork, especially his herpetological designs — boa constrictors, Russell's and gaboon vipers, mombas, pythons, anacondas, moccasins, garden-variety earthworms, for a humorous touch. Rattlesnakes were especially in vogue, by virtue of the tattooist's use of the gonads as rattles. Suddenly, virtually every male on campus was sporting a multicolored snake on his snake, which, naturally, tended to render the trend passé.

Then, one night at the frat house, while he and his brothers were initiating pledges in a totemic ritual circle jerk, all of them naked to the bone — their ophidians — every one required to perform fellatio on the other ten, Cobra Man was struck with a brilliant vision, which would return him to his former glory, on first being fitted with his genital serpent. He'd submit to a higher form of reptilianism: he'd enlist the body piercer at the tattoo shop, who normally installed barbells, rings, and studs in ears, noses, eyebrows, lips, navels, nipples, to split his tongue an inch back from its tip, thus enhancing his spitting-cobra persona, increasing his sexual prowess, shamanistic powers.

Within a week of having it sliced, after the pain subsided and healing was complete, he began wildly flicking his tongue. In a matter of days, girls were again queuing up at his door. His frat buddies were forced to issue timed tickets.

After three nonstop days, Coby called for a moratorium. He needed a little time to recuperate. His lingual and priapic units had suffered neural fatigue; their muscles had turned to rubber. But the clamor for Ted Apted's services continued even in his temporary absence. Never had any of the girls experienced such spirituality.

By the time Cobra Man was ready to resume, he discovered, to his dismay, that he had stiff competition. Just as before, only much sooner, the *sui generis*ness of his gifts had been knocked off. Now, anyone could raise his snake to striking position, flick his forked tongue in salacious excitation.

But still Coby stayed a step ahead. Asked to orate at graduation, he took the stage, opened his mouth, and began speaking in tongues. For ten minutes, the thousands at commencement listened with beguiled inspiration, until they started writhing, climaxing, drenching themselves.

Seafood Buffet

Finding and securing the errant well-worn leather port-
folio wasn't all that monumental. Anyone with half a con-
science would have done the same. After all, it was in plain
sight, perched atop a stainless-steel trash receptacle in the
building's drafty garage-level vestibule. He spied it immedi-
ately, upon coming off the elevator from the fifteenth-floor
dining club, where he'd just finished stuffing himself on a
seafood buffet.

His response was automatic. He related to another's
despair, the anguishing soul who'd misplaced his life's work.
Though he'd never been in that boat, he could empathize.
And this was a chance for him to perform a good deed, a
mitzvah, if you will (he had many Jewish friends), turn this
lost item, so vital to someone, into a blessing.

He felt somewhat like a burglar, taking the case, but he
was positive it was the right thing to do. He'd hate for main-
tenance to trash it, have it fall into bad hands. It would be
safe with him, in his apartment. He'd call the owner once
he got back home, to his high-rise. Surely he'd be able to
determine to whom the thing belonged.

As good fortune would have it, he found a business card
inside; it was a lawyer's. He dialed the number of the firm,
left a message, though he didn't expect to get anyone on a
Friday night. The offices were located two floors below the
dining club, where he'd glutted himself on lobster, crab,
shrimp. He left his name, his home and work numbers,
then went to bed, feeling damn good about himself. Dreams
failed to materialize, which meant all was at peace.

To his surprise, he didn't hear from the man — not
Saturday or Sunday. He drove out to his own office, to
check his messages.

Monday morning (he waited until 9:30, since lawyers,
like bankers, were notoriously slow starters), he called

again, raised a switchboard operator, who, though admitting she was three weeks new on the job, expressed her dubiety; she didn't recognize the name. After a silence, she confirmed that her list showed no such person. With saccharine politeness, she assured him she'd ask around, let him know if she heard anything.

He tried to find the man in the phone book, but there were at least ten pages of Smiths, and so many of them carried initials or variations — Christian name and middle initial and vice versa. He really had no stomach for ringing nearly two hundred people, didn't want to impose upon their privacy, had no patience for that kind of thing. And he had work to do.

By Thursday, late afternoon, having heard nothing and growing a bit uneasy about possessing something not his (he'd purposely not pried far, into the contents), he contacted the building where he'd found the portfolio. Yes, they had a lost-and-found department, but, no, there weren't any reports of an item matching his description.

After the third week, he almost forgot about the case. It sat by the sink, in his kitchen. Within another month, it had become invisible.

It wasn't until he attended the next seafood buffet, which was an anticipated semiannual event at the dining club, that the portfolio came to mind again. Be damned if the exact same situation didn't occur, when he exited the elevator, from the fifteenth floor, stepped into the vestibule, bordering the basement garage. There, before his eyes, like a taunt or an insult, atop the trash receptacle, perched a similar case, beckoning his attention, begging him to assure its safety.

He seriously considered walking right past it, out the door, but that same old conscience compelled him to pick it up, take it home, open it, with hope of returning it.

Once back in his kitchen, he unlatched the portfolio and found a business card identical to the other one.

No more seafood buffets for him.

Reborn Again, Again

Now, here it is, not just another but a not-so-nother Monday mornin' neither, and Redbird's is still buzzin' from yesterday's beevehide o' pigskinizations. Everyone in the joint, from Cookie down to Gert 'n Tracy 'n Michelle, includin' the Cathlick table, two tables o' Bible-readin' freaks, 'n various strays 'n regulars 'n such, can't stop jawin' about how we pulled this one clean outten our asses, how fuckin' lucky we was, 'n how old Mr. Anthiser's Bush just mighta had the last laugh as well as the last say-so. Guarangoddamn-teeya, he done had my last say-so, which wasn't too goddamn shabby neither, if you acquire the drift o' my not-so-drafty Bud brewskies.

Yesterday, bein' Sunday, if the May-hen 'n the hula-hoopla over to Fubar's was any indications o' the excite-ments that'd been buzzin' this sportin' town-of-all-towns up 'n down the Missus Sloppy all week, and 'specially yester-day afternoon, like ten zillion bees buzzin' the beevehide to get a personal crack at the queen bumblerbee's hide, if you catch the lash o' my driftin' draft's whip, then all's I can say is that I'd hate to ever get caught in the jaws of a starvin' lion or dead center in the eyes of a hurrycane, when it's headin' for Miami's Beach.

I mean, things was so crazy comin' up on yesterday's pigskin tug-o'-war monster-truck tractor pull between our St. Louis Cardinal Rams 'n the Tampon Bay Fuckaneers, who done boated up from Tampon Bay in the Neverglades on their pirate ship to play us, here in our downtown TWAT Dome, for the championchip o' the NCF league division.

Fack is, I couldn't sleep all week, had a tight chest, like someone done stuck me in a huge vice grip and squeezed so's to flatten me to a crisp, like them scrap-yard composters that takes a whole car in their jaws to onced and, within seconds, turns your Cutloose Supremes or Dodgem Rumblers into the size of a White Crapper hamburgler patty. And fack also is that me 'n my buddies tried like hell to come up with four tickets to the TWAT Dome, but at anywheres from five hunnerd up 'n down, best we done come up with was four o' the most bodacious seats in Fubar's twat stadial of underaged babes, get them seats smack-dab in the center o' twenty-five units all blarin' to onced, get 'em by gettin' there yesterday, of a Sunday mornin', at 10:01, when they opened their doors, and parkin' it there from 10:01 to 6:40-somethin', when they done wrapped up the victorian speeches 'n all the hula-hoopla o' the second game on national TVs, and I wrapped up 'n down (more down than up) my last victorian toast too.

But the first game, between the Jackoffville Cougars 'n the Ten o' Seas Titan Oilers, didn't really mean shit to no one over to Fubar's, since all that mattered hadn't happened yet, which was how bad we was gonna whup up on them Fuckaneer pirates from the Neverglades, only by the time we got to kickoff time, me 'n Brotherton 'n Bobbit 'n Kowalski was so loop-d-looped with brewskies 'n chili dogs up the ass 'n fully loaded tater skins (Fubar's whips up the meanest fully-loaded tater boats known to man; it's their speciality, with secret ingredials, only I done had so damn many o' them spuds mackenzials over the years I know exackly what goes into the works — bacon tit-bits, cheddar cheeses, greened onions, a ton or two o' pure lard butter, for taste, 'n half a delivery truck o' soured creams ... I mean, even the missus's guanamole chip-'n-dip spread don't quite cut the mustard, come up to Fubar's fully loaded spuds boats) 'n nachos with mountains o' cheddar cheeses drippin' from their pores 'n more brewskies by the longneck (the four of us toughs, by the start of our game, coulda pooled our bottles, melted 'em down, and made all the windows for a eighty-story skyscraper) 'n a constant reorder o' steamin'-hot giant pretzels smothered in cheddar cheeses 'n then, by the start of our game, another round o' three chili dogs for each ones of us . . .

I mean, if we wasn't in our elementals 'n primals for primal-time TV play-off pigskinizations, I don't know what would be, and on tops of all that chow, my heart's begun poundin' as they interduce our boys in the TWAT Dome with them fireworks fillin' up the stadial with smoke (you could smell it all the way to Fubar's, or else it was Fubar's own volcano o' cigarette smoke, which was thick as elephump dung, which you couldn't cut with a mashiti or a ginseng knive or spread with a snow blower neither).

Anyways, I couldn't begin to believe the first play — we done won the coin tossed and selected to receive with 'n against the winds, 'cause even in the covered stadial, it was ten hurrycanes goin' with 'n against the grains, for people screamin' so loud they used up all the oxengen in the air and had to set artificial oxengen fans goin' just to keep the half-million payin' fans alive . . . anyways, here we're inspectin' to see a instant replay o' last week's game against the Vikin's, where we tore 'em a new hole on the first play with a massive, colossial pass from Captain Kirk Warners to Bruce Isaac, only this time, Captain Kirk, believin' he's gonna unleash another o' them zip-a-dee-do-das to Bruce Isaac, like a total asshole, throws a massive, colossial intercession to one o' their big Fuckaneer goons, which, in less time than it takes a fired-fly to light up its ass with kerosene or some such, commences to mess up a touchdown and settle for a field gold, all in a matter of a minute, which stuns the TWAT Dome to stunned silence and stuns all o' Fubar's and all o' St. Louis to a stunstill, and now my heart's poundin' like a herd of elephumps tryin' to stay eight steps ahead of a jungle forest fire.

I don't know if it was eatin' all that grub or combonations o' the grub 'n the brewskies 'n the worker bees in them snatch-high short shorts 'n barely less'n skimpy blouses flyin' in 'n out, deliverin' their honey to our pots, and me wishin' if I wasn't with the boys that I could get pollinized as well as ripped . . . but whatever it was or wasn't, the game kept gettin' more 'n more duller 'n sleepier 'n (I can't even believe I'm sayin' nor thinkin' it) *borin'* as all hell, 'cause we was the ones gettin' the major whuppin' up on, if you catch my draft. Who'da guessed from all the speed 'n stuff we got on our team that we'da been totally shut down? It was like drivin' a eighteen-wheeler into a milelong quicksand bog with a hunnerd-ton load o' raw cesspool sewage in tow — I mean the major shits, so that if it hadn't been for a bad hike from center that went over the quarterback's head from the shotguns that done gave us a touchedback with two points and receivin' of a free kick, which is a punt from a standstill, we'da had a measly three points, which we got instead o' scorin', on a mighty wobbly kick by a guy with a bum settin' leg.

As it was, we went into the halftime lockup, after thirty minutes o' play 'n another sixty or seventy o' stoppinages for ads, winnin' by two ignint points — five to three. I mean, this ain't a whole lot better'n a ten-dollar tit-lick over to Q.T.'s. Fack is, it's about like pissin' in the Neverglades, which, come to think on it, must be filled with gators 'n crocs 'n gars, 'cause you could see the writin' on the balls, which erection the game was headin' — and I don't mean into the lockup room for halftime . . . more like down the tubes o' the biggest toilet known to man- 'n womankine combined alike.

I mean, come the hell on. Here you got the most implosive offense in the history o' pro pigskins, or almost, and we can't mustard up or down more'n five points in thirty minutes. And on top 'n bottoms o' that, we come out and start in commencin' to play the same lame game and find ourselfs, right aways, suckin' hine tits, losin' five to six, which spells doomsday 'n a-pack-o'-lips over two, or so we're thinkin'.

By this time, my buddies is startin' to get boysterous, outten frustrations 'n disgusts 'n aftershocks, like me, myselfs, 'n me, and we see all our celebatin' drainin' out 'n away by the minute, the play, the fuckup, 'cause them Fuckaneers is obvially for real and ain't goin' away nor gonna lay down in the middle o' the roads to the Georgian Frontier and play possums or anything else but "for keeps," which is really beginnin' to piss me off 'n on and make me sick, though sick could be from downin' 'n drownin' too much grub 'n brewskies outten unnervousness, 'cause we could see the whole season comin' to a abruptive end . . .

'Til, now, it's under four minutes to play, and Captain Kirk, whose name we done now renamed Captain Jerk-off, throws to a guy, a white guy (fack is, the most amazin' thing to all of us is that boths pitcher 'n catcher, for a change, is both white) for a hell of a amazin'ly lucky catch in the end zones, which brings the score to eleven to six, which means our Cardinal Rams is gonna try for a two-point conversion kit, which they commence to fuck up, which means that with four minutes to go, the Fuckaneers can make a touch-down and beat us thirteen nor twelve to eleven, which is real scary and brings the entire TWAT Dome to more silence than it's got even when it's empty, 'cause them Fuckaneers start comin' down the field, after our kickoff, poundin' away at us like they're gonna get a touchdown real easy — our linebackers 'n safeties keeps fallin' down, playin' off them pass runners too much, and our blitzers keep misguessin' the runs from the passes 'n such.

Then, wouldn't you know it, almost like someone in Mr. Anthiser's Bush's boredroom done sent down a bribe to the replay referee . . . be goddamned if the Fuckaneers don't catch a pass that brings them within our twenty-yard line, with only ten yards to go for a first down and three downs to do it . . . be damned if this ref don't call for a instantanial-replay ruling on the catched pass that John Madman replays on TVs and scribbles up at least ten times, showin' the pass was perfeck 'n above boards 'n stuff . . . be damned if the ref don't overturn the call 'n John Madman, too, and call the pass uncomplete and send the Fuckaneers back to second 'n twenty-some-odd on their thirty-fifth, which they commenced to blow and give the game to us in the last seconds, just by pure luck o' the iv'ry — iv'ry, 'cause here's two white guys, Captain Kirk 'n Rickley Parole, both Southern Babtists from the sounds of 'em in the postgame innerviews, who done already pulled, just by the shortest o' their short hairs, the eleventh 'n a half hour miracle Heil Mary outten the bag, which done had the entire TWAT Dome goin' more berserk than a hunnerd 'n eighty deciballs per hour, which is louder'n bein' tied to the tail of a 669 jet on takeoffs . . . both guys pullin' the ram's sheep's wool over a almost entirely black pack of pirate Fuckaneers — for that matters, these was almost the only two white guys on the Cardinal Rams neither. . . .

But what gets my ass is here we is in Fubar's watchin' all the May-hen down to the stadial, and me thinkin', "Jesus, this here's a Merica! This here's St. Louis! Sombitch! Ain't we great, gettin' to go to the Stupor Bowl in Atlanta's Georgia!" And Fubar's is just about as crazy as the stadial for all them underaged dropout waitresses tryin' to jump 'n hump the payin' fans, huggin' 'n humpin' 'n bumpin' 'n grindin' on each other like gay lesbian femalian fagnits 'n screechin' 'n poppin' all them blue 'n yellow balloons hangin' from the ceilin' and us still watchin' them TVs with Coach Dick Vermillion 'n Bruce Isaac 'n Captain Kirk 'n Rickley Parole all called up by Terry Bradslaw to say a few words nor eight 'fore they go dancin' around the Asstroturfs, holdin' up the Halas's Comet Trophy, Captain Kirk sayin' how much he wants to thank *Jesus* for givin' him this victory today, thank *Jesus* for makin' it possomable for him to quit stockin' Presildent Bush's beans 'n hash 'n corn 'n such onto the shelves of a Iowa Piggly Wriggly so's he could work his way down the ladder through the Canadial 'n Europeal pigskin leagues before comin' to St. Louis, thank *Jesus* for makin' him the star that he is, *Jesus* for makin' everything in the whole world possomable, includin' his beauteous wife 'n mother, who's sittin' there in the stands tryin' to pretend they're bein' extra immodest, knowin' all them cameras is on their mugs, thank *Jesus* for makin' the planet, makin' St. Louis, makin' the TWAT Dome, thank *Jesus* for teachin' him to thank *Jesus* for thankin' *Jesus* for thankin' *Jesus* (thank you, *Jesus!*), and then, oh, yeah, Captain Kirk forgets for a minute to thank *Jesus* and axeldently remembers to thank the St. Louis fans, with me bein' one big bodacious example o' the millions who don't unnecessarily believe that *Jesus* made me what I ain't 'n isn't, is 'n wasn't, won't 'n will 'n never shall be. . . .

And still, no one in the stadial's leavin' the joint — I mean, all them freak-fagnits wearin' blue-'n-yellow-camelflage pajamas 'n body paints 'n masks 'n ram's horns stickin' outten their heads 'n arms 'n asses, and wavin' sponged rubber noodles 'n towels 'n stuff, and Kowalski 'n Bobbit 'n Brotherton 'n me clankin' together another round o' longnecks over here to Fubar's as a final send-up 'n over, each of us wonderin' who's gonna be the undesignatal driver, 'cause none of us's in any pre- or postgame condition nor shapes nor whatever neither to drive home on our owns, let alone call our wifes to come get us . . .

'Til, of a suddlenly, I start seein' rams like crazy, white-fleecy 'n black-nappy-headed rams, rams leapin' fences, rams leapin' off precilpisses, rams leapin' over half a thousand moons all with white fleeces 'n ram's horns, moons, that is, all wantin' to mate with the rams I'm seein', 'til I'm down on the floor, closer to down 'n out than down 'n in, seein' moons 'n stars, not rams, not football ram-stars neither, but regular stars 'n moons, the moons n' stars that come up before all the lights go out, them stars 'n moons not givin' a good hoot in hell that I'm about to turn the lights out on 'em, the entire day too, 'cause we done won the ACF or the NCF (I can't never get them names straight) and us on our ways to the Stupor Bowl, the St. Louis

Cardinal Rams, that is, and me 'n my three best buddies in the whole hamisphere on our ways to the most ripped-roarulous Stupor Bowl tailgate key party we never did dream — at my house again this year, after a year's layoff on probational for fuckin' up the missus's Xmas Eve cele-bation for me bein' neglectful n' unselfish 'n late over to Q.T.'s for a pre–Xmas Eve celebation o' my own – and all I know is that St. Louis is reborn again, again, like Captain Kirk 'n all his teammates on the good ship *Innerprize*, which is the one I think I was on right then 'n there in Fubar's, yesterday around 6:40-somethin', goin' down into otter space for the count in a flame o' stuporous-bowl glory.

On the Decline and Fall
of the Species

This bitter six-thirty-Saturday a.m., he debates which newspaper he'll take from which mechanical vendor — *St. Louis Post-Dispatch*, *Wall Street Journal*, or *USA Today*. By anyone's lights, this is an adequate variety from which to choose one's poison. But his debate with his world-weary psyche really ranges beyond the peripheries of this decision.

In reality, he doesn't want to read even one more column inch of barbarity, be informed of another hijacking, kidnapping, train derailed by a drunk driver, white-supremacist beheading or dragging of a black, high-school shooting by wimp-commandos, berserk-day-trader massacre, subway gassing, abortion-clinic bombing, xeno- or homophobia-motivated homicide.

He's literally sick to his soul and tired as hell of being assaulted, daily, by evildoing. It's all too much for him, how societal savagery has become a way of life, like rush-hour traffic and gangsta rap.

From what he's recently read about a new study, even Neanderthals — our Darwinian Adams — regularly practiced cannibalism, ate their families and friends, with impunity, which lends support to his growing malaise, if, in fact, this word actually describes his distress. All he knows is that reading a rag, *any* rag, is proving to be increasingly contemptible, as one morning blends into the next, without regard for his sanity.

Reaching into his pocket for quarters, he suddenly remembers the slugs he's brought to clog the slots — the news-box terrorist.

Hair

He awakened to strange volcanoes erupting all over his face, from follicular craters.

At first, he was certain it was severe acne visiting his physiognomy, an affliction that would leave hideous scars, nothing more, nothing life-threatening, just an ugly puss, hardly an obstacle to successful socialization.

But to his visual mystification, when he went to the john, gazed into the mirror, he was stunned to discover the truth: he was experiencing a facial-hair spurt, a shaggy big bang. Whether it was a product of hormones or nightmares, the fact of the matter remained that, overnight, he'd sprouted a bodacious beard, one worthy of both cough-drop Smith brothers.

Why? How? He hadn't the slightest clue. When he tried to mow his course, with his formidable three-blade Norelco, the razor stalled in the density. Even if it had been a Dixie Chopper, it would have choked on his cheeks' rough, sputtered out in his protruding nasal thickets, on the rough and fairways of his neck, the brows and lashes surrounding his eyes' lakes.

He arrived, at work, lucid, competent, willing. By noon, though, not only had the facial hair returned, but he was now being smothered in fur — even his forehead, lips, tongue, palms, fingernails, navel, penis, buttocks, anus, heels — growing faster, by far, than Mississippi kudzu.

When the five o'clock claxon wailed and he realized he was still drawing breath, he drove directly to his tonsorial engineer, convinced her to shave him naked as a pink baby, as if depilating his entire body might somehow discourage further outbreaks. She did so, out of respect for his patronage, not to mention the potential kinkiness (she didn't have a problem with modesty).

That night, he slept like a debarked log, knowing his

skin was as glossy as a dolphin's, as smooth as a bowling lane's hardwood.

But while a red sun rose in the east, he awoke to find he was triple his normal size, with hair. He didn't dare go to work, for fear that he would be misunderstood.

By noon, he'd begun overheating. After dousing himself, for hours, in a cold shower, he felt enough like his old self to get dressed, walk to the ice-cream shop. The lady who scooped his rocky road took his money, wished him a "very good day." But no matter how hard he tried, he couldn't get the treat to his mouth.

Disconsolate, he shuffled home. His hair having dried in the sun, puffed out, he could no longer fit through his front door.

He went around to the backyard, lay down supine, in the man-high grass, and became indistinguishable from nature.

The Merchant of Pornlock

Once upon a time out of time, a traveling salesman from Pornlock knocked thrice, then banged, upon my door, finally broke into my tidy cottage, where I was in the throes of composing a poem after Samuel Taylor Coleridge's "Kubla Khan."

Startled from my reverie, I inquired indignantly and with mortification as to his business, his importunacy, his reason for violating my privacy. All he could tell me was that his mission was of origin divine, requisite to my joy.

Grudgingly, I gave him my divided attention, allowed him to present his wares, hoping they might spur further creativity. But he wasn't peddling opiates, just "marital aid" paraphernalia and apparatuses — your run-of-the-mill orgasm facilitators.

For nigh on forty-five minutes, I endured his passionate, high-pressure spiel, trying to resist his insistent appeals, until, weary and wanting to complete my poem, I succumbed to his transparent wiles, purchased two dozen spotted Persian dildos, a baker's dozen of Turkish pocket pussies, and five boxes of self-lubricating French ticklers, just to get him out of my hair, that wanton merchant of Pornlock, who distracted me from capturing the full fantasy I'd dreamt in a laudanum-induced trance, which I was deeply appreciating, a vision far beyond any of Timothy Leary's.

What chutzpa that salacious sexmonger had! And what a sad consequence for the world, his intervening on my psychedelic "Kubla," which I sensed would be life's Rosetta stone. Alas! The poem's to-morrow is yet to come.

But I do have something to show for the loss: a pleasure dome of erotic accouterment.

Grave Premonitions

Lately, succubi have been swarming his sleep, like flies dive-bombing a horse. His tossing and tumbling in the sheets are the overheated nag's tail swishing in vain; his unconscious scratching of his face is the plug's ears twitching, to little avail.

He's trapped between nightmare and tranquillity, a victim of the waking day's dead, rising, like waterlogged flotsam, to slumber's oily surface, from the depths of a thousand yesterdays, swarming with green flies, gnats, fleas, bees, bats.

Surely it's not his job causing this affliction of Biblical dimension. If so, he'd have reached that conclusion easily, been the first to size up his options, retire or quit in a New York minute, seek employment as a night-shift embalmer, if for no other reason than to avoid having to sleep evenings. But in truth, he's never considered his occupation hazardous to his mental health. After all, how harmful could it possibly be, inspecting cemeteries for the state, updating the census of headstones, listing grounds conditions — erosion, brown grass, weeds — reporting canted, broken, or vandalized markers graffitied with hammers and sickles, swastikas, Stars of David driven through with scimitars, investigating dug-up plots, rifled caskets?

Actually, he's found his tasks rather peaceful. Many of his sojourns are in country towns — enclaves of 250 or fewer souls — or in Kansas City and St. Louis. Often, he's the only one alive in the potter's fields. The drives are relaxing, too.

For almost forty years, he's experienced *joie de vivre* on the job. But of late, something pernicious has been gnawing to the core of his contentment; something perfectly mortifying has been disturbing his sleep for weeks. Of one thing he's absolutely certain: he's got to get some relief from these visitations.

Even though he believes in spectral phenomena, it isn't in his scope to suspect that ghosts, provoked by his innocuous meddling in the line of duty, could be at the bottom of his troubled slumbers. That's too stupid, too inane an excuse to explain why horseflies (those winged mares of the night) dive-bomb his dreams, sting his eyes and ears, bite his body — succubi swishing their bat-o'-nine-tails, lashing his psyche with grave premonitions.

Stupor Bowl 34 x 2 + 1

Part One

Slept clean through the major 'n minor parts o' Monday, clean as a bear in a cave o' snowy Sundays, if you acquire the drift o' my paw prints in the sands o' time. Fack is, I bet half Saturn 69 done called in sick nor didn't even bother, like me, 'cause me 'n the boys already done put Alferneeze on notice Friday afternoon there'd be no way we was gonna make it in day after the Stupor Bowl. I mean, come the hell on. That's just uncommon knowledge. 'Specially when our own St. Louis Cardinal Rams is in the shootout.

Anyways, I didn't (call in, that is), which was fine, 'cause I needed to recupinate from the most splendickulous tailgate key party ever known to man on the face o' the maps. I mean, Jeezus! . . . But suddlenly, I can't even hear myselfs thinkin', 'cause them mackerel bastards is goin' at it like a pack o' highrenas on a zebra's dead carc-ass, still goin' on about the game, two days later, which I can't say I don't blame 'em, but so fuckin' loud 'n stuff they almost make me forget my headsnake, which's gotta be about a two-hunnerd-footer for wrigglin' through my brain all the ways from Sunday night to this Tuesday mornin', here in Redbird's. I mean, this thing's gotta be the most bodacious Boeing restrictor in nor out o' craptivity.

"Boys, I still can't believe this has happened to us. First, we get Mark McGwire hitting seventy homers; now Kurt Warner takes us to our first-ever Super Bowl."

"Tell me! And you know what? We even got to see a bunch of white guys get to play, for a change — on Tennessee's team, at least."

"Yeah, even with a black quarterback, to boot."

"But wasn't that Steve McNair great? Ran us ragged, I'd say."

"Almost tore us a new one, with that final play."

"How about old Georgia? Is she a *piece* of work, or what? Seven husbands and a half-native Indian, with Stetson, boots, and a ponytail, for a *body*guard."

"Howard, you forgot to mention she's an opera star too."

"You mean retired chorus girl, don't you, John?"

"For my money, she should've sung the national anthem, instead of Faith Hill."

"Yeah, to the tune of 'Coal Miner's Daughter' or 'Crazy.'"

"It's an unlikely lot, I'll grant you that."

"Thanks, Sid."

"No. I mean it. What you got there is a bunch of over-the-hill, alcoholic excoaches and a front office that's got ties to the mob, guiding a bunch of Seventh-Day-Adventists-Charismatics-Born-Again-Televangelistical-Southern-Baptist-Leadership-Fellowship-Councils-of-Southern-Athlete fanatics in shoulder pads and tearaway jockstraps."

"Whoa, Sid. Rein in your Clydesdales . . . all sixteen of 'em."

"Well, it's true, according to Kurt. Those eleven guys on offense and their coach, Vermeil, are the twelve apostles."

"When did Kurt Warner tell you that, Sid?"

"Hey, John, Howard, Bud, cut me some slack. That's what these guys think. What you've got here is Kurt Warner as John the Baptist and his whole flock. I mean, these guys have come again in the flesh."

"Whoa! Whoa, Sid! It's gonna be all right. It's just a game."

"Yeah, Sid. And I suppose Marshall Faulk and Isaac Bruce are Peter and Paul."

"And Kevin Carter and Ray Agnew are Matthew and Luke."

"And I bet you're John, John, right?"

And by this time, I'm beginnin' to get my bearin's, here in Redbird's, beginnin' to catch the drift o' them snapper-bastards' draft, even though it ain't easy for havin' to fight barehandled a two-hunnerd-foot Boeing restrictor just so's I can tell my ham-'n-mushedroom eggs omlit from my hand. Come to think on it, bet I could drown out this headsnake, slinkin' around in the sewer pipes behine my forehead, with one good brewsky — I've heard pythons 'n vipers 'n such can't swim.

"Tracy, hon, bring me a brewsky — Mr. Anthiser's Bush's best Light in the house, just to drown down Cookie's eggs omlit this mornin'."

"Anything you say, hon, but . . ."

"No butts, Tracy. I need to take a bite outten the hair o' the snake's dog that done bit me Sunday night."

"Some game, huh, hon?"

"Oh, yeah. Some game, all right. Me 'n the boys over to my house for Stupor Bowl 34 x 2 + 1. I mean, bodacious to the tenth power plus eight, if you acquire my drift."

"I got your drift, hon, and I'm goin' to get your draft right now."

But just about the time Tracy done brung me that sweaty bottle o' brewsky and sets it down on my table, which I begin to pour with a hand that ain't all that steady, so's that my longneck clinks the chilled mug, them snappers from over to the Church o' Saints Velveeta 'n Lindbergher 'n the Fat-Cat Bastards o' the Fattycan Council o' Pigskinizations . . . them loudmouth, holier'n-them-'n-thou religional sympalthizers start in again on that stuff the idiot they call Sid, for some stupid reason, done first mentioned.

"Sid, where'd you get all this contempt, this indignation toward your fellow man?"

"John, what *is* that?"

"Hatred, Sid. Your acrimony, your animosity, your rancor, your antipathy toward your co-religionists in Christ."

"Whoa, yourself, John. I can't even understand you. Are you saying that I'm intolerant, a bigot or a racist or something?"

"No, Sid, I'm just wondering what's wrong with those guys believing in Jesus. Don't we preach the same thing, every Sunday, in Mass?"

"That's just it. I don't think *we* go around making a huge public deal about it, do we?"

"I don't know, Sid. Didn't the Pope make a pretty good splash right here in the TWA Dome? I mean, who could've missed him?"

"And who was right there at his feet?"

"That's right, Howard — Mark McGwire, himself."

"Yeah, well he's Catholic."

"So what, Sid? He's a great athlete."

"Which means what?"

"Sid, I guess it means that all great athletes have to believe in something higher than their own gifts. I think it's an athlete thing, a kind of modesty, a way of allowing for miracles."

"What's that mean?"

"Well, what I mean is, if you have faith, you can believe in miracles, and if you believe in miracles, you might just end up with a guy (who, five years ago, was stocking grocery shelves in Iowa) playing ball for a coach (who, until a few years ago, was retired from coaching football for fourteen years) hired out of desperation by a chorus/call girl with blonde hair and seven husbands and a shitpot load of dough, who just happens to have the same name as the Dome, where all of them ended up, Sunday night, winning the Lombardi Trophy by about the length of the one outstretched hand that just missed crossing the goal line, with five seconds to go, to take the game and the momentum into overtime for what most likely would've been a Titan sudden-death victory. . . . That, Sid, is what I call a miracle of miracles, and if it takes thanking Jesus in front of sixty thousand fans and two hundred million TV watchers, who's to say that Kurt Warner might not just *be* Jesus come again in the flesh?"

"Jesus, John. Whoa! Rein in *your* Clydesdales, too."

"Whoa, yourself, Sid, Howard, Bud, Dan, Tom! I'm talking miracle of miracles, miracles of Biblical proportions. Here you got a guy, a quarterback who believes in Jesus, like he's got a bee up his ass, a bee telling him that if he *bee*lieves, really *bee*lieves, that bee will let him win the league MVP and take his team to the Super Bowl, where he'll also win the Super Bowl MVP, all in one year, if he only quits his grocery-store-stock-boy job and goes to play eight-man, indoor Arena League football, then goes to Europe, to play with the Amsterdam Admirals, before coming back to the States to be bumped around until he lands here on the most losing team in the whole league, ends up as the third-string quarterback to a great star, who, in a preseason game, blows out his knee, so that they have no choice but to make him a starter . . . if only he'll *bee*lieve that the guy he throws the winning miracle pass to in the Super Bowl, a black guy from Fort Lauderdale (who also *bee*lieves in the power of Jesus just as hard as he *bee*lieves), Isaac Bruce, not Jesus, is the go-to guy, who will help him save the game, save the day, save St. Louis from infamy, ignominious defeat . . ."

"What? From *what*?"

"From losing their asses in the final two minutes after dominating the entire first half of play."

"John, boy. Hold up. Don't you think . . . ?"

"Think what, Sid? What I think is if Isaac Bruce wants to *bee*lieve that Jesus kept him from buying the farm when his $200,000 Mercedes blew a tire two months ago, driving home to St. Louis, from Columbia, with his girlfriend, turning over and over without a seatbelt, and that Jesus made him catch that improbable pass from Jesus himself, who am I to deny him his *bee*lief, even if we Catholics like to take a lower-profile approach to miracles, like the miracle of turning wine into the blood of Christ and the miracle of turning a wafer of bread into Jesus' body at Holy Communion? Listen, miracles are miracles, any way you slice and drink them."

And me thinkin', the only miracle I'm gonna need this mornin', beside the miracle that'll turn them asshole, fartbag, loudmouth, mackerel-snappin' Cathlick bastards from the Saints Velveeta 'n Lindbergher pinnochial school for fagnits 'n altered boys into souls 'n such that done left their own dead-ass bodies, silent ghosts 'n livin' deads 'n such that done quit the Earths for a eternity o' forevers, which is so far beyond 'n behine my thoughtful thoughts to inconceive . . . the only miracle I'm gonna pray for, this two-hunnerd-foot-headsnake Tuesday mornin' after the most disunbelievable Stupor Bowl victory of ever 'n all times, is the miracle o' the brewsky I'm havin' right now I'm hopin' is gonna turn a two-hunnerd-foot Boeing restrictor into a two-inch trouser worm, so's I can get my own dead ass to my hydraulic wrench on to Alferneeze Johnson's line, over to Fenton, along with three other miracles, which is that, somehow, my buddies Kowalski 'n Bobbit 'n Brotherton find their ways into works this mornin' too, as well, and also, which takes me back to what a great Sunday afternoon we done had over to my rump room with my three good buddies 'n our good-sports wifes, good sports for not only endurin' us celebatin' but particilpatin' in the postgame celebatin' of us winnin' our first Stupor Bowl of all times.

Lucifer Nosferatu

When is emptiness the equivalent of fulfillment? After he's sucked the blood from the carotid artery, grown drunk on the seductive sediment escaping the defunct chambers of the thumping heart that gradually ceases its pumping, pumping, and become comatose from tonguing the crimson puddles that collect, like red rain, in the foggy streets of Ossuary and Far Necropolis.

After all, his sanguivorous appetites require him to tap the sap from the tree of life, drain the veins of the most robust hosts, either by needle or fang — he's not particular as to the "type" of his nourishment or the method of extraction and collection. Whether his samples are tainted or pure matters, at the end of the day, not at all.

He's a greedy, insatiable beast — no bones about it. He's the original hematic misanthropist, with an amazingly sadistic capacity for inflicting affliction (call it relish for the morbid, scrofulous, macabre), who's known no stopping, no calling it quits, since his disgraceful fall from grace, his improbable bid to be God.

He's decidedly not picky — neither a beggar nor a chooser is he. When it comes down to choosing winners and losers, he always picks the latter, thumbs down, belly up, and gladly sucks (so to speak) hind dug, cuts much slack for each new generation of Nosferatus who move into his neighborhood, to check out the consanguineous action.

His fulfillment derives from others suffering that empty feeling in the pit of their guts. It's his high, the rise in his Levi's, his commitment to publish Rushdie's *Satanic Verses*, his desire to give Jesus Christ his first blow job, so that history might record, for posterity, how Lucifer paid lip service to God and sucked the blood of the Lamb.

Devoted to Your Job

Just the other day (was it the lady who cuts your hair, or was it your attractive new personal trainer, who puts you through your paces, with free weights and flexibility exercises that approximate yoga with a trace of pseudo-Zen, or was it possibly one of the three waitresses who alternate serving you at the neighborhood café, who address you as "love" and "dear" and "hon" despite having no personal contact with you other than to dish up your "same ol', same ol'," egg whites cooked without grease, toasted bagel ("hold the butter"), decaf ("no cream"), since they appreciate you making it easy for them — your habitual abstemiousness, which they call "regularity" — or was it maybe your exquisite "assistant," the recent college graduate imploding with Vesuvian vitality, breasts disproportionate to her diminutive features, which could give a petrified tree a hard-on, whom the office manager assigned to you and three other distribution agents in your section, to help you surmount your Mount Suribachi of paperwork, with a semblance of organization, a degree of expertise consonant with company policy?) . . . just the other day (or might it have been a month ago, last year, a decade back, perhaps never?), one of the ladies who slip through the cracks in your life made an overture, spoke a body language you might have interpreted as sexual innuendo, an invitation to initiate a relationship, or she didn't — you're just not sure, this morning, sitting here at the café, in your regular's chair, fending off the "hon"s and "love"s and "dear"s, filling in your mental calendar with the week's activities: haircut, Tuesday; weight and flexibility training, this afternoon and Thursday, at 4:45; your quarterly requisition/disbursement report, due on the CEO's desk Friday, sans fail.

All you *are* certain of is an uncertain loneliness that turns your devotional hours and days into monks floating from atrium to nave, rectory to refectory to bed, in your soul's cold cells, via cloisters connecting you to the job you've held fully fifty years.

Sleep Mode

One night last week, tomorrow, tonight, or never, after arriving home from a late tryst with lambent shadows cast from streetlights planted, like trees, in front of his urban apartment, shadows razoring his eyes and the sidewalks, whose mica-flecks blinded him with midnight's dangers, he couldn't triangulate his location relative to the state-of-the-art computer he kept in his bedroom, always humming in "sleep" mode, ready to help him elude dream-demons — a handy amulet, like a high-tech garlic necklace, to divine and ward off vampires. In fact, he hadn't even been seeking sleep when he got lost in cyberspace.

For reasons too curious to second-guess, he was so frightened by what he'd just seen on his stroll (the ritual to which he'd rigidly adhered for the last two decades of his protracted bachelorhood) that he repudiated sleep altogether, entered his friendly eBay portal, through AOL, and immediately proceeded to attend auctions in progress, scrolling through, viewing, coveting expensive rarities. (He had a predilection for Amphora portrait vases, Raoul Larche bronze sculptures teeming with captive, naked femmes fatales, Art Nouveau candelabras, compotes, tazzas from the turn-of-the-century WMF German works, with their sensual, sinuous efflorescence.)

But for the life of him, literally, fantasizing himself one of the new Internet billionaires, with unlimited disposable income to spend on da Vinci's sketchbooks, ten van Goghs, five Monets, Einstein's original holograph notes for $E=mc^2$, made no sense to him whatsoever. And not once did he ever click his mouse to execute a bona fide cyberbid.

Whatever might have been lurking in the shadows on the streets outside his apartment, one night last week, tomorrow, tonight, or never, mortifying him to such a frenzy he couldn't sleep, slowly dissipated as he auctioned himself off, safe with the highest bidder.

A Literary Hero

Yesterday, during a lull in my daily labor of reconfiguring masterpieces of world literature, I contrived to convince my supervisor I'm still purposive, worthy of being deemed a productive person, a model, fully conforming citizen-cipher, whose existence the state must continue extending, by handing out my latest résumé touting my political affiliations and intellectual achievements — my fifty years of rewriting Homer and Shakespeare, Cervantes, Dickinson, Dostoevsky, and Faulkner, for Mother Dystopia-Urania.

But instead of distributing it, I hurled it into the wastebasket in my rented cubicle, located on the third level of Chamber Six, Labyrinth Four, our national archive for printed and electronic information . . . hurled it into a general-issue 3A shredder/trash can, along with a five-year accumulation of manuscripts from my current classified project — feeding the *Odyssey*, Rig-Veda, Pentateuch, and Upanishads into the Class 9 SS (Super Secret) Molotov-Stravinsky Collator-Scrambler mainframe, to create the *State's Definitive Bible for Human Survival.*

Needless to say, when rumor infiltrated Labyrinth Four, from which I'd bolted, twenty-three minutes before lunch recess, obliterated my Manhattan Project, the sirens and claxons and shrill electric oscillators turned the complex into an ear-fracturing Bedlam. Of course, using their MRI wall scanners, they found me, within seconds, hiding inside a reeking dumpster on the loading dock, hoping to escape to the landfill, where, amidst the scraps of my incomplete Bible, I might die in peace — the people's literary hero.

Stupor Bowl 34 x 2 + 1

Part Two

So now it's halfways into the mornin' and the cladder 'n shriekin' 'n arc welders' flashes is givin' me a major multigrainer on top o' this two-hunnerd-foot headsnake, and to combat the dizzies, at the break, I swig down some hooch I got hidden in my lunchpail to take the edge off, which it does, just long enough for me to huddle with my buddies, who is all, like me, hung way over 'n out, knowin' we just had the best Stupor Bowl party man, femalian, 'n beast coulda ever done hoped to see and us tryin' to rehash the double gargantulous Stupor Bowl party we done had over to me 'n the missus's castle, just up from Mr. Anthiser's Bush's brewery, off Sidney 'n Broadway . . . me thinkin' back, 'cause none o' the other three's really got squat to say to each others, nor to me neither, thinkin' myself all the way back to Sunday, thinkin' how this is the party o' the millennial, the new millennial, which is scary, since we got 999 more years and the thought of already havin' the best the millennial's got to offer is enough to make a guy think his lucky stars he's alive 'n kickin' in 2000, wonderin' what "it's all downhill from here" really means — is this the one 'n ownliest Stupor Bowl we're gonna celebate with our team? Should we maybe call Stupor Bowl Sunday off permanally after this game? . . .

"Hey, Bobbit, can you believe we've had four chances to stick it up their holes, bury their asses in the first half, and can't do shit from Shinolaville?"

"Sucks, don't it? I'd like to see the score twenty-one to ziplock by now."

"Man, but can that Kirk Warner hurl a pigskin, can't he?"

"Yeah, he should be able to — he's had a ton o' practice tossin' them Kotexas 'n them Charmin' TP cartons 'n Dranos, back in Iowa's Piggly-Wriggly's best."

"That time he done spent in the Arena League didn't hurt him none neither."

"Brotherton, who's gonna win this damn game?"

"Jeezus! If the Cardinal Rams don't do somethin' damn soon, we're dead meats."

"For sure, we ain't gonna win off the stump-leg kicker we got, if we gotta rely on field golds 'n extra points 'n such."

"Ain't no extra points when you ain't got no TD's — and that don't mean Ted Drewes."

"Kowalski, you got that to a T 'n a D."

"T, shit! D, shit! I'd like to see somethin' other'n ads on top of ads."

And me thinkin', what a time we was havin' watchin' the game draw more closer 'n closer to a close, 'til we done had so many brews 'n so much dogs 'n chips 'n pretzels 'n guanamole chip-dip 'n Frito-Laid tostados 'n junk foods, 'til the four of us roughs (the wifes was in the kitchen, preparin' the continuable feast, jawin' away, not even interested in the games, which is unpossomable for me to believe), us watchin' our team suck hine tits, lose all its gas 'n steams, lose its momentals too, 'til them Ten o' Seas Titan Oilers done close the gap o' the sixteen points we done scraped up outten somethin' close to thin airs, 'til you could feel the game goin' over to them bastards.

"Jeezus, what a bunch o' fuckin' bums we is."

"Bums, shit! Us Cardinal Rams is castorated sheeps."

"And, boys, we're watchin' our team piss good piss after bad piss — we're in 'n down the crapper, which is where I gotta go right now, quicker'n quick, so if you guys'll just exsqueeze me while they're runnin' this ad for Superman, showin' him walkin' again after he done broke his back ridin' one o' them Collidesdales, I'll be back in a Jiffy Lube."

Of a suddlenly, we're all screamin' our asses off. Captain Kirk's done just hurled a whole carton o' Charmin' TP seventy yards down to Bruce Isaac, who done commenced to make a noncatchable catch catchable and hightailed it on into the end zones.

"Jeezus! Did you see that?"

"Holy shit!"

"Shit over two to the seventh power plus two."

"Fuckin' A! Our Cardinal Rams done just pulled the Big One clean outten their asses."

"Talk about clutched balls, and with less'n two minutes to go."

"Man, that Kirk Warners's some piece o' work, ain't he? I mean, what balls 'n guts 'n tits that guy's got."

"And what a babe of a wife, too. See the way he goes over after a game and kisses her right in front o' the whole whirl?"

"Yeah, if it was me, I'd be jumpin' her bones right in the stands."

"Yeah, and I'd be jumpin' on for a late hit, even if they called a fifteen-yard penalties."

"Yeah, and I'd probably be OK with her mother. Fack is, mother almost looks younger'n the daughter — damn good-lookin' babe herselfs."

"Jeezus, Kowalski. Ain't you got no taste, that you gotta rob the graves?"

"Yeah, I got taste in my pants, and its name's Die-Hard-On Johnson, baddest one-eyed jack o' diamonds in the mines o' North 'n South Afurca."

"Oh, yeah, then what the fuck you want with Captain Kirk's mother-in-laws? Who you want, then, is Bruce Isaac's girlfriend, Shequina Noxema Pond's Cream o' Some Young Guy."

"Listen, Bobbit, right now I wouldn't feel too shabby if I got your wive's tailgate key for the night."

"Well, fuck you, Zeke!"

"And fuck you too, Jack! I could probably be OK, too, if I got to open up the gate to your ol' wive's tail with her nookie's new key, too."

"And we'll just have to see what we'll just have to see,

won't we, come time to throw the house keys into the Rams' horn-hat tonight."

"That's right, guys. But right now, we ain't got this game won yet, like I thought, 'cause we're cavin' in on another indefensible collapse."

"That fuckin' George Eddy's a fuckin' moose over two, ain't he?"

"Nothin' but a tank could stop him . . . nor maybe a goddamn purple Saturn."

"Somebody catch that crazy nig, McHair. There he goes again. Jeezus, he runs like a guy who done just stole a case full o' jewelry outten JC Pennay's."

"What kind o'shit's *that*, Brotherton?"

"Cow shit I know?"

"Bare asshole Mary, she'll toilet to you."

"Boys, them Titan Oilers just called time."

"How much time?"

"How much time'd they call?"

"No, asshole, how much time they got left after the time they done called runs out?"

"Five seconds."

"How much they got to go to tie us?"

"Seven points."

"No, asshole, how much yards they gotta gain to get into the end zones?"

"Ten yards."

"Uh-oh. We're douched."

And then that play o' plays, tackle o' tackles, miracle o' miracles, when our black guy, Mark Jones, done tackled the outstretchin' hand o' their black guy, and the TV keeps focusin' in on that hand tryin' for all its might 'n lion's share o' the mane to shove that little pigskin over the line 'n into the end zones for a tyin' touchdown, which he *don't* — that hand gonna stay there, stretchin' out for 999 more years, makin' this the best hang-on-from-in-front, pull-pigeons-'n-crows-outten-your-magicianal's-hat's-ass-'n-turn-'em-

into-peecocks-'n-peehens-o'-paraldise-or-some-such pig-
skin game that ever done been played, 'til us guys is goin'
so berserked 'n crazy with the glorious dizzies o' victory,
you'da thought us four roughs was Bruce Isaac 'n Captain
Kirk 'n the Jones guy, who done the save-the-millennial
tackle, 'n Coach Dick Vermillion, me bein' the coach, natch,
since I'm hostin' this year's Stupor Bowl 34 x 2 + 1 tailgate
key party over to our house — me 'n the missus's, that is,
doin' the hostin', natch.

And me seein' it's now way passed ten, closer to ten-
thirty by the time we pop some more brewskies and chomp
down a dozen or three more dogs and watch all the con-
feddi 'n speeches comin' down in Georgia's Frontier Dome
and Captain Kirk tellin' the whirl Jesus done won the game,
not him, not the other players neither, not the coaches 'n
such neither, not the St. Louis fans neither, and us not
listenin' to all that shit, 'cause we know that's just Captain
Kirk's thing, and us all sensin' it's gettin' down to our own
two-minute warnin' and that we gotta pull some peecocks
'n peehens outten our own magicianal Rams's horn-hat by
throwin' in some house keys and hope our own miracle o'
miracles miracalize after the miracle-o'-miracles Stupor
Bowl victory of our miraculous St. Louis Cardinal Rams.

"Guys, there's one change in this year's rules, beside us
bein' able to ask for as many instantanial replays as we want."

"What's that?"

"It's that my old lady 'n me wants you three guys, 'n
womb-so-never your wifes for the night's gonna be, to stay
right here to home with us. Kowalski, you 'n your bride-
to-be gets our bedroom. Bobbit, you 'n your helpmeat-in-
waitin' gets your choices o' the dinin' room or the livin' room.
Brotherton, you 'n your missterious lady-o'-the-night gets
either the livin' room nor the dinin' room, whichever comes
first nor last, five years nor sixty thousand miles on your
drive train, if you catch my drift. Me 'n the lucky young lady-
in-'n-outten-waitin', whose tailgate I get to open . . . she 'n

me, myselfs, 'n me gets to stay right here in the rump room, on the hide-a-sofa, to tidy up the place, sorta, and finish up all the leftovers 'n -unders, so to speaks, if you catch the drift o'my miracle whips."

Look on the Bright Side

For the last five nights, possibly a week, maybe a month, a year (you're unclear, for the constant buzz in your ears, which drowns out your hemispheres' intercom, those voices that communicate with you, through hidden speakers), you've not eaten dinner.

It could be from a chronic lack of hunger, short long-term-memory loss, the strict dietary dictates of an occult weight-loss program, or your protests against the powers in the universe that limit your control over chaos to a few emotions and codes.

You're too weak, these days, to question your fate, justify destiny's inscrutable ways to man — to yourself, at least — and even if you could, you know better than to speak for your fellow human beings.

Suffice it to say you've not eaten dinner in a while, and leave it at that, so as not to call undo attention to your condition. After all, you seem adequate to the task — maintaining, that is, keeping soul, if not body and mind, together — and bemoaning your woeful state could land you in drearier circumstances; you could be missing breakfasts and lunches, too, until even your ghost would give you up.

By now, you should realize that being dead creates necessary inconveniences but that starving isn't really one of them. Be grateful for small favors; you could still be alive, eaten by Alzheimer's.

Inhumantity

One day, out of the clear blue, too abruptly to be "of a sudden," something truly confusing happened. He ceased seeing other people as human beings, began perceiving them as ants.

Why ants instead of dolphins or armadillos? Why lowly pismires, not apes or monkeys, which surely would have been closer to him in both body structure and mentality? He couldn't begin to say. Even aardvarks and anteaters might have been preferable to his sensibility, but he had little, if any, control over his psyche. If ants were what his mind had chosen as a queer substitution for humans, so be it.

The problem was, since childhood, he'd been terrified of all varieties of insects: mosquitoes, moths, beetles, mantises, lightning bugs — you name it, he'd get the willies, hives, when anything, especially spiders or ants, crawled on him.

Moreover, he'd never particularly thought of himself as disdainful of mankind. Quite the contrary, he'd always admired *Homo sapiens* not only for its upright stature but brain capacity — civilization, wisdom, religion its greatest gifts to the planet.

So why, one fine habitual morning, he should awaken to the vivid realization that he was surrounded by ants, he hadn't a clue. Driving to Spivac's for breakfast and arriving weirded him out, without a doubt. In every car he passed on the highway, he could clearly see, in the drivers' seats, bulbous black heads with bulging eyes and antennae. The waitresses at the local café were scurrying in and out of tables, on six legs, delivering plates of omelets, hash browns, griddle cakes, with their two front legs, to customers who were sitting in chairs, their waists bent between trunks and metasomas, chewing with mandibles and maxillae.

Curiously, when he focused on his own hands, they were light-skinned, hairy, unchanged — human. What was going on was beyond, beneath, him. Indeed, he was the sole human in a land of *giants* — pismires, that is.

When he finally got to the factory, his coworkers on the assembly line filed right past him, gave him the silent treatment; in fact, they were standoffish all day — something he'd never experienced on the job. It was almost as if he were too ugly, too foreign, too big. None of the ants operating the robots, wielding welding torches and pneumatic tools, watching gauges, spoke a sound to him, or if they did, he couldn't hear them — not for the din but for their subliminal language, one unintelligible to his ears.

He finished out his shift, staying to himself, then drove home, stunned, mortified, wondering what tomorrow would bring. He'd never felt so excluded, marginal, alone. Always he'd been the gregarious type, never a pariah. That night, he burned his TV dinner, went to bed after watching a *Three Stooges* film.

On waking, he felt a tidal wave in his sheets. Then the wave tingled his face. Six-legged creatures were marching, goose-stepping, over his chest and belly, infesting his pubic hair, turning his penis into a throbbing erection, a colony of ten thousand scaling his legs, weaving in and out of his toes, exploring his ears and nose, crawling behind his eyes, inside his mouth, under his tongue, down his esophagus. He was subdued, couldn't rise, couldn't move.

By noon, there was nothing left of him, nothing to carry off, not even his endoskeleton. (His apartment showed no signs of forced entry.) On his pillow lay one tiny supine ant, twitching.

Pea Brain

On the twenty-eighth day of an early-millennium May, when he awakened consummately late and went to locate his mind on the nightstand, where he'd placed it beside his false teeth and glass eye, on retiring to bed after his duties as Inspector of the Sky, he couldn't, for the life of him, find it, his mind, which he always removed from his cranium, at day's end, and fastidiously stored in a used coffee can he was equally methodical about changing and refilling, weekly, with a mixture of Listerine and chicken-and-matzo-ball soup.

As was his habit, he popped the plastic lid immediately upon stirring from blank-slate sleep, to ensure that everything would proceed apace, from reinserting his full dentures and right eyeball to completing his toiletries, dressing, only to be stunned: his robust encephalon had wizened to the size of a raisin and was stuck to the bottom of the Folgers Mountain Grown tin. The preservative had somehow leaked out or evaporated (the carpet showed only the same old stains). He'd been called "pea brain," but this seemed ironic.

Despite seeing the telephone, with his one good eye, he couldn't think about using it to summon help. By sheer conditioning, he picked up the raisin, inserted it under the retractable flap of skin that covered the cavity in his trepanned skull, and felt only ever-so-slight electrical impulses, vibrations.

Gradually, his heart began to stir, his blood churn, his body grow warmer, suppler, his muscles reflexive. But he quickly noticed that all his functions were slower, operating at perhaps one-eighth their normal rate.

Work would be a daunting undertaking. He'd do his best, make the necessary excuses, muddle through until break, when he'd have his first chance to visit the parts department and be fitted for a new mind.

He hoped they still stocked his model.

Einstein

Recently, in *JAMA*, *USA Today*, and *Scientific American*,
he read that his intimate affinity with the common human
being is beyond question, in fact is a reifiable absolute,
given that 99.4% of his and people's DNA is identical, their
double-helix amino acids are compatible.

And this verifiable certainty has blown his mind to
smithereens. For decades, he's suspected that a connection
exists between his own species and man, that *Homo sapiens* isn't so advanced, after all, that *Planet of the Apes* is
more fact than fiction.

Tonight, he swings from bar to bar, in his cage, seemingly satisfied with his new status as equal, a chimpanzee
with the potential of Einstein, similar, down to the wrinkles
and hair.

Nonetheless, he's outraged by evolution, which has
relegated him to third-world/class citizenship, a mere simian who could be sent into space or used for experiments
in labs.

Tomorrow, he'll awaken at daybreak, dangle and brachiate, by his fingers and opposable thumbs, in the canopy
of his habitat, screeching, babbling like a newborn person,
as if reaching out to overleap the chasm of ages, touch you
and me, his long-lost family, the branch that apes him with
inane mockery.

Stupor Bowl 34 x 2 + 1

Part Three

I can't hardly believe my ears, but sure's rain makes snow, pigs make bacons 'n ham steaks, one from one equals one, and bears shit in the Tiger Woods, them Cathlicks, all six of 'em, includin' that fat bastard they call John or Jack-off or asshole or fucknuts, is actually in some kind o' silent mode, which may be 'cause they're grievin' the news from last night that Dick Vermillion done quit, got out while the get-outten's good, done took his Stupor Bowl decoder ring 'n all his trophies 'n bonerses and caught the red-eye outten the Cardinal Rams's camp while the getting's too good to not resist. Whatever, it's hump day at Redbird's and my Boeing restrictor's done gone back down to the size of a ant or a termhite dyin' of uninterest — in other words, it's beeswax as unusual 'n abnormal, and in about a hour, I'll be back out to Saturn 69, bustin' my hump just to keep up.

But hump day's hump-day-dump-day to me, and all that falls down picks itselfs up and gets its shit together again, just like I do after every vacation 'n holiday 'n weekend, pigskinizations nor not, 'cause in this great cuntry, there ain't no quittin' 'less you're sixty-three 'n your name's Dick Vermillion and you just done won the grandpappy of all granddaddies in the pigskin shootout and can now afford to say, "Been here, done that," as they say, and say, "Enough's enough, already," which I ain't ever gonna get the plea-sures o' sayin', 'cause Stupor Bowl is Xmas 'n Thanksgivin' 'n birthdays all rolled up into one big gumball, and thems only for the extra lucky 'n the filthy rich 'n for religional guys who believe in Jesus 'n God 'n witches 'n livin' deads 'n Christ 'n Pope Piles 'n miracles 'n such.

But I don't got no squarrels with none of 'em, 'cause no one's guarangoddamnteed shit in the first 'n third 'n firth

o' froth places to boot. Truth is, I gets my share o' the a
Merican dream-team pie, if you acquire my drift, the good
ol' a Merican hair pie, that is, which, truths be told, is the
warped whift that makes the whirl go 'round . . . ol' Ms. a
Merican Hair Pie, which, I gotta emit, is about as good as it
gets when the getting's good, which it was this passed
Sunday night, when my bestest buddies in the hole whirl
was over to the house, celebatin' our most amazin' Stupor
Bowl victory over the Ten o' Seas Titan Oilers. I mean,
Jeezus! Where but in a Merica can you have a hunnerd or
two guys all geared up to beat the livin' shit outten each
other, so's two hunnerd million fans can get their rocks off
doin' nothin' but gettin' their rocks off watchin' a bunch o'
TV's 'n eatin' their fat asses off 'n fuckin' their brains out,
which is their way o' sayin', "Right on!" "Bust their chops!"
"Break their backs, snap their necks, smash their schlongs!"
"Punch out their eyeballs!" "Rip off their balls!" "Shove that
pigskin up their rectals 'n outten their fire hoses!" which,
face it, is a man thing, definitely not a femalian thing, guaran-
goddamnteeya, which, after all these years o' takin' advan-
tages o' my old lady, who trusts 'n loves 'n counts on me to
bring home the rent 'n the futilities 'n the car payments, I
know, first-, second-, 'n fifth-underhanded?

So sorta knowin' what I know and sorta lovin' my old
lady pretty fuckin' much for puttin' up with all my abnega-
tional immortalities 'n unoriginal aboriginalites, nor some
such, I done took a few libertarians in the week priors to the
Stupor Bowl by sneakin' over to Q.T.' s on one o' my lunch
breaks, where I just happened to have a mission, which was
to see if I could contrack Julie No-Name 'n Dakota 'n two
o' their good buddies to see if they'd be willin', for the
price of a ticket to the post-Stupor Bowl game over to
south St. Louis, not Atlanta's Frontier, for four General
Useless S. Grunts a *piece*, which adds up to eight hunnerd
fat ones for the lot of 'em, a week's worth o' my boltin' down
motor mounts over to Saturn 69 after taxes 'n such . . . if

they'd be consensual to come over to my place and help me, myselfs, 'n my three good buddies celebate the only Stupor Bowl we're ever likely to ever win, which they agreed hands off 'n down to do on a dime, a dime worth four General Grunts a *piece*, which is precisely what they done did come Sunday night, and I do mean *come*, 'cause the best thing that happened was that by the time us roughs was gonna sacraface our lovely virginial brides to each others, them gals from over to Sauget showed up on my porch steps and announced they was there to collect their General Grunts.

"Was General Grunt to home?" which I said to onced, "Of horse," 'cause Dakota, if not Julie No-Name, reckelnized my old lady, 'cause she done spoke to her when I gave out last Xmas Eve, over to Q.T.' s sportin'bar and she had to help, in her G-throng 'n all, put me in the truck my old lady done drove over acrost the river to collect what was left o'me.

So them gals show up in their performance gear, only now they're all in yellow 'n blue, blue throngs the sizes of a rubber band, no tit covers, 'n yellow on their nipples, and, believe this or not, their beardless clams half yellow 'n half blue. I mean, cold as it is, here they is, the four of 'em on my porch's doorsteps, and how can I refuse to let them home-less strays into the warmth of our happy Stupor Bowl castle-home? And true to their callin', all I can say is, despite all my carefully laid change o' plans, "Here the four of us is" (our wifes done took refugement in the bedroom), Bobbit in the kitchen with Julie No-Name, who's got the longest, most sexiest seventeen-year-old legs you ever done seen (that lucky fucker — Bobbit, that is, not her, damn sure, 'cause he ain't exackly no prize in the bottom o' the Cracker Jack-Off box, if you catch the drift o' my draft); Brotherton in the laundry room (how in hell he ended up on the floor between the washer 'n dryer I'll never know) with the most gorgaceous sixteen-year-old cunt I never seen, with amazin'-

grace guavas that'd be amazin' on a elephump twiced her
sizes, 'n a full growth o' hair (which surprises me, since Q.T.'
s tries to run a clean establishments, if you catch the clip o'
my drift's clit); Kowalski with about a overaged fifteen-year-
old, flat-chested beauty with the blondest blonde Klondyke-
gold hair on top 'n a bush o' red saffron rice down below,
like a rain forest o' chili peppers, who kept tuggin' at his
pants 'n shirt as they wandered off to the garage, then
ended up on top o' the ridin' mower, nekkid as brush apes,
fuckin' like they was minkies just discoverin' their missions
in afterlifes for the first time in the chain o' bein'; and me,
still down in the rump room, doin' my damndest to make
sure my old lady don't peek down the stairs and catch me
in my birthday leisure suit . . . me so excited to see Dakota
again, who I ain't mated since Xmas Eve a year ago, and me
congranulatin' myselfs for makin' all this work out just fine
for one week's salary, me sparin' our old ladies from havin'
to give in to what *USA's Today* calls unexspousable abuse-
ment (which is pure bullshit), that I couldn't even disbe-
lieve how great the sex is with Dakota, who I can't even
disbe-lieve's fuckin' my brains out in my own house, celebatin',
her friends with my friends, my bestest buddies with her
stagehands, who, my bestest line buddies, I guarangoddamn-
teeya, ain't never gonna have a second chance at another
Stupor Bowl victory, now that ol' Dick Vermillion done
packed up 'n picked up grubsteaks, the four of us gettin'
laid of a Sunday night in my own house with four o' Q.T.'
s finest. I mean, Jesus P. Fuckin' Christ on a Copper Crotch!
Guarangoddamnteeya, even ol' Captain Kirk Warners his-
selfs ain't havin' this good o' time tonight, celebatin' with
his wife-in-Jesus 'n his mother-in-laws-in-Jesus, too, maybe.

Jeezus! This here's a Merica! And us roughs deserve this
specialized treatment. I mean, ain't everyone, nor just any-
one neither, who can grow up in a Merica, in St. Louis on
the Missus Sloppy, and know there ain't no pigskin team in
the whirl that's got a legs or two up on us. I mean, sombitch!

This here's the Midwest — the hairy armpit o' the Hardland — but it's our Midwest 'n it's our Hardland, and I can only tell you that we may be hairy armpits 'n groins 'n hard-ons 'n such, and we may only know how to brew brewskies and slap Saturns together from Jap-scrap, but we sure as shit know how to whup the livin' tar babies outten any other pigskin team in the whirl in 2000, which may just be the way it goes for the next 999 years — or it may convert, after to-night, back to our shit pigskin teams o' the seventies 'n mid-nineties, kinda like Cinderelish's pimpkin that done got squashed by the fagnit stepsisters, pissed 'cause Cinderelish got in the poison prince's purple pants, while all they got into was about a busted glass sneaker over two.

Whatever 'n nonetheless 'n however 'n whatever 'n anyways, all I gotta say is that a Merica is one bodacious land to be from when all you can do's bolt down motor mounts and fuck the most gorgaceous six-foot Dakota in eighteen states and know you can wake up the next mornin' and go to work with a clear unconscious, knowin' you ain't left no babies in your wakes, 'cause them gals know how to take care o' theirselfs . . . go to work knowin' you done got a clean slade with your old lady, too, 'cause she's just glad as shit, fat as she is, that she didn't have to put out for no Bobbit nor Kowalski nor Brotherton, any one o' which coulda as easily been in my bed Stupor Bowl night as me (even though I wasn't in there neither for bein' down in the rump room, tidyin' up 'n stuff with Dakota), 'cause we been doin' this for the last ten years, tradin' partners, that is, every Stupor Bowl 'cept for last year's, when the missus done caught me red-handled over to Q.T.'s on Xmas Eve with the very same Dakota, who just could be Queen of all Stupor Bowls for all times — Dakota that is, not my wifes.

And me here in Redbird's of a post–Stupor Bowl Sun-day, hump-day Wednesday mornin', not with a care in the air, nor headsnake neither, anymore, thinkin' that every day in a Merica, no matter its Babtist Jesus-freak quarterbacks

'n its mackerel-snappin' Cathlicks, 'n no matter its chorus-
gal pigskin team owners with seven bleached-yellow heads
for seven husbands, 'n its black pigskin wive-killers, wearin'
them Bruno Magics, 'n its white, Offal-Office-underaged-
fuckin' Presildents, 'n no matter its blue-ring-around-the-
collar workers over to Saturn 69 . . . every day here in a
Merica is Elvis the Pretzel, Karla Mae Fucker, Tricky "Dick"
Nigson, 'n Big Mike McGwire; every day here in a Merica is
Bud Light years beyond any other Third Whirl land 'n any
other planet on Earth, and that, in a shell o' nuts, is the cat's
pussy, guarangoddamnteeya.

I mean, where else but in a Merica can a guy pledge his
love to his old lady, his energy to his nig line boss, his friend-
ships to his assemblage-line buddies, his St. Louis Cardinal
Rams's horns to the most bodacious nekkid babe over
acrost the river to his favorite sportin' bar, and keep his
nose above boards 'n under the gun, his chin clean, and his
head still treadin' water in a cuntry that makes Madagascan
'n the Maluccas 'n Bozzoslobovia 'n Crotchkneea 'n Sizzley
look like they ain't gonna come alive for the next five hun-
nerd years, at least?

I mean, this here's a Merica, and I'm fuckin' glad to be
alive 'n kickin' 'n fuckin' my old lady 'n Dakota — if not
boths on Stupor Bowl night, then one night apart. Som-
bitch! Sombitch! I mean, miracle o' miraculous miracles! If
this ain't what miracles is all about, then miracles ain't
bodacious. St. Louis kicks ass! Saturn 69 kicks serious ass!
Ol' Dakota's delicious clit kicks stupendickulous ass! And
since Dick Vermillion's adios to the Cardinal Rams sucks
hine tit, I guess I'll be doin' the coachin' from here on outs,
startin' with callin' our next practice over to Q.T.' s sportin'-
bar TWAT Dome, with me 'n Dakota 'n Julie No-Name tryin'
out for next year's Stupor Bowl team — me, myselfs, 'n me
hopin' to edge out Captain Kirk Warners for a birth on the
good ship *Innerprize*.

The Man Who Would Have Daphne in His Bedroom

Last weekend (or was it? He's not even certain, anymore, for the blur that pain has created in his brain), while helping to load into his station wagon a bronze statue of Daphne he'd just bought in a neighborhood antique mall (the Belle Epoch *objet d'art* three feet tall, seductive in its patinated, diaphanous draping and its mythological redolences of pure classical beauty, pedestaled, perfect for his bedroom, to accompany him into dreamy sleep), he miscued. When the store attendant lending a hand let go of the hundred-pound sculpture's onyx base, he strained his lower-back muscles, trying to keep from dropping its head on the blacktop, doubtless saving it from a fatal fracture.

He realized, at once, from the ominous snap, that he'd done something grievous to his lumbar — nothing less, if he was suffering the least of all evils, than a week's recuperation for a second's ignorance or, better expressed, profound stupidity.

After all his years of hunting and gathering, hauling home weighty baubles, bibelots, *arts decoratif* (call his roses, no matter by what other names, junk), he should have been more careful.

Even now, though it's been five days, he's still paying for his blunder in spades. Doomed to stay in bed, stiff as a cadaver, afraid even to twitch or sneeze beneath the sheets, he only engages the physics of ambulation to reach the john, pissing and shitting while standing up in the shower stall.

Cursing his curse, he wonders if he's turning into a laurel tree.

Promenading with Mr. Versace

Sometimes, late at night, when he's out walking his
fourteen-foot boa constrictor (its vestigial hind legs and
hip bones protruding slightly, in an exercise of evolution-
ary futility), which he keeps on a rhinestone-studded leash
attached to a custom-made collar and muzzle he special-
ordered from the local pet shop, the snake capable of
undulations calibrated to keep pace with his four-mile-an-
hour stride, the snake, Mr. Versace, at complete ease with
its surroundings and with its master's nocturnal routine,
oblivious of streetwalkers and common hussies, sophisti-
cated odalisques pimped, in stretch limos, by the mayor
and his Council of Concerned Teenage Mothers, who would
proposition "Mr. V" for an hour's venery, if only its owner
would become a consenting adult . . . sometimes, when the
moon is bright in the seventh house and he and Mr. Versace
(a South American boa of Italian ancestry, whom he acquired
from an aging member of the Medellin cartel, retired, "with
extreme prejudice," from brokering contraband coca ex-
tracts — the snake a token of the man's lasting appreciation,
his deep esteem for their Colombiano/Gringo *amistad*)
are very much in Shakespearean love with each other, he
thinks about his life B.C. (Before Constrictor) and weeps
for all that he realizes, now, he was, without the slightest
insight then, missing out on, when he misguidedly had only
a wife and three children, houses in the Hamptons, San
Francisco, Palm Beach, and Corfu, mistresses from Rio de
Janeiro to Juan-les-Pins, a stable of racecars, and a seat on
the Bourse de Paris . . . sometimes, when summer rains
drench his contented soul or snow blows his mind with its
exquisite flakes or a total eclipse of the sun exposes him
and his lover to its midnight nuclear corona, he runs his
fingers down Mr. Versace's cold-blooded spine, massages
the boa's vertebrae, ribs, anoints its dry scales with aphro-

disiacal emollients, pleasures it by peeling its molting skin, and whispers the sweetest nothings from his own flicking tongue, knowing, as they both know oh too intimately, that after concluding their promenade, their undulation, they'll return to his chichi digs, bed down in a cage he's had custom built by Moen, approximating a rain forest in Brazil, and, squeezing each other with voluptuous passion, consummate the holiest union between man and snake since Creation.

Jurassic Gas

Once upon a time, you roared and wreaked mayhem, dragging your fifty-foot tail behind you. How could you not have guessed that of apatosaurus you were immaculately born? Indeed, you should have, and in the end, you did.

For your entire plodding lifespan, you paced back and forth, doing your damnedest to terrify trifling mankind, make it realize the pettiness of its paltry wars, festering animosities, and xenophobia.

You imagined humans would have gotten a clue, left off their intolerance and greed long enough to unite in a protective brotherhood, subdue and defeat you. But they were too stupid, too self-absorbed.

Long after they atomized their planet, withered into near-extinction, you plodded through their irradiated ruins, marveled at the desolation of lifeless ash, hungered for prelapsarian vegetation.

But such was not your luck, to glut on greens. You too died a shabby, ignominious death. In the end, you and your fifty-foot tail powered a Ford Explorer for six miles, until it ran out of you.

A Modest Proposal for the Radical Extermination of Words from Our Lexicon and a Reversion to Gesticulation as the Lingua Franca of All Discourse Public, Private, and Otherwise

How can I ever find the words to say "Thanks" or "I love you" or "I appreciate your patience, your understanding, your willingness to let me have the freedom to be myself, reinvent myself, do what I need to do to reach my full potential, actualize myself"?

How can I ever find the words to say "Enough!" or *"Basta!"* or "I've had it!" or "I'm mad as hell, and I can't take it anymore!" or "I give up, cry uncle, refuse to take one more step in any direction" or "I'd prefer not to" or . . . or . . . "oh, fiddlesticks! I quit!"?

How any of us ever finds the words mystifies me. Despite the *OED* cataloging of half a million, in all their glorious etymologies and first uses, we rely, unless we're professors or lexicographers, on fewer than five thousand of them to express our urges and primal desires, not to mention ineffable epiphanies.

How we ever found the words in the first place is the most amazing perplexity of all. Imagine the original caterwauling and babblement that, one day, awakened from inarticulation and accidentally learned to pronounce "naked," "innocence," "snake," "tree," "apple," "Let's fuck."

How can I ever find the words to describe "God" or "miracle" or "forever," when my fundamental distrust of words reminds me that people double-talk out of both sides of their assholes?

I propose this final solution for words: transplant all tongues from mouths to hands.

Biographical Note

Louis Daniel Brodsky was born in St. Louis, Missouri, in 1941, where he attended St. Louis Country Day School. After earning a B.A., magna cum laude, at Yale University in 1963, he received an M.A. in English from Washington University in 1967 and an M.A. in Creative Writing from San Francisco State University the following year.

From 1968 to 1987, while continuing to write poetry, he assisted in managing a 350-person men's-clothing factory in Farmington, Missouri, and started one of the Midwest's first factory-outlet apparel chains. From 1980 to 1991, he taught English and creative writing at Mineral Area College, in nearby Flat River. Since 1987, he has lived in St. Louis and devoted himself to composing poems and short fictions. He has a daughter and a son.

Brodsky is the author of fifty-one volumes of poetry (five of which have been published in French by Éditions Gallimard) and twenty-three volumes of prose, including nine books of scholarship on William Faulkner and seven books of short fictions. His poems and essays have appeared in *Harper's, The Faulkner Review, Southern Review, Texas Quarterly, National Forum, American Scholar, Studies in Bibliography, Kansas Quarterly,* Ball State University's *Forum, Cimarron Review,* and *Literary Review,* as well as in *Ariel, Acumen, Orbis, New Welsh Review, Dalhousie Review,* and other journals. His work has also been printed in five editions of the *Anthology of Magazine Verse and Yearbook of American Poetry.* The Center for Great Lakes Culture, at Michigan State University, selected *You Can't Go Back, Exactly* for its 2004 award for best book of poetry.

Other poetry and short fictions available from TIME BEING BOOKS

YAKOV AZRIEL
Threads from a Coat of Many Colors: Poems on Genesis

EDWARD BOCCIA
No Matter How Good the Light Is: Poems by a Painter

LOUIS DANIEL BRODSKY
You Can't Go Back, Exactly
The Thorough Earth
Four and Twenty Blackbirds Soaring
Mississippi Vistas: Volume One of *A Mississippi Trilogy*
Falling from Heaven: Holocaust Poems of a Jew and a Gentile *(Brodsky and Heyen)*
Forever, for Now: Poems for a Later Love
Mistress Mississippi: Volume Three of *A Mississippi Trilogy*
A Gleam in the Eye: Poems for a First Baby
Gestapo Crows: Holocaust Poems
The Capital Café: Poems of Redneck, U.S.A.
Disappearing in Mississippi Latitudes: Volume Two of *A Mississippi Trilogy*
Paper-Whites for Lady Jane: Poems of a Midlife Love Affair
The Complete Poems of Louis Daniel Brodsky: Volume One, 1963–1967
Three Early Books of Poems by Louis Daniel Brodsky, 1967–1969: *The Easy Philosopher*, *"A Hard Coming of It" and Other Poems*, and *The Foul Rag-and-Bone Shop*
The Eleventh Lost Tribe: Poems of the Holocaust
Toward the Torah, Soaring: Poems of the Renascence of Faith
Yellow Bricks *(short fictions)*
Catchin' the Drift o' the Draft *(short fictions)*
This Here's a Merica *(short fictions)*
Voice Within the Void: Poems of *Homo supinus*
Leaky Tubs *(short fictions)*
Shadow War: A Poetic Chronicle of September 11 and Beyond, Volume One
The Complete Poems of Louis Daniel Brodsky: Volume Two, 1967–1976
Shadow War: A Poetic Chronicle of September 11 and Beyond, Volume Two
Shadow War: A Poetic Chronicle of September 11 and Beyond, Volume Three
Shadow War: A Poetic Chronicle of September 11 and Beyond, Volume Four
Shadow War: A Poetic Chronicle of September 11 and Beyond, Volume Five
Rated Xmas *(short fictions)*
Nuts to You! *(short fictions)*
The Complete Poems of Louis Daniel Brodsky: Volume Three, 1976–1980

866-840-4334
http://www.timebeing.com

HARRY JAMES CARGAS *(editor)*
Telling the Tale: A Tribute to Elie Wiesel on the Occasion of His 65th Birthday —
Essays, Reflections, and Poems

JUDITH CHALMER
Out of History's Junk Jar: Poems of a Mixed Inheritance

GERALD EARLY
How the War in the Streets Is Won: Poems on the Quest of Love and Faith

GARY FINCKE
Blood Ties: Working-Class Poems

ALBERT GOLDBARTH
A Lineage of Ragpickers, Songpluckers, Elegiasts & Jewelers: Selected Poems of
Jewish Family Life, 1973–1995

ROBERT HAMBLIN
From the Ground Up: Poems of One Southerner's Passage to Adulthood

WILLIAM HEYEN
Erika: Poems of the Holocaust
Falling from Heaven: Holocaust Poems of a Jew and a Gentile *(Brodsky and Heyen)*
Pterodactyl Rose: Poems of Ecology
Ribbons: The Gulf War — A Poem
The Host: Selected Poems, 1965–1990

TED HIRSCHFIELD
German Requiem: Poems of the War and the Atonement of a Third Reich Child

VIRGINIA V. JAMES HLAVSA
Waking October Leaves: Reanimations by a Small-Town Girl

RODGER KAMENETZ
The Missing Jew: New and Selected Poems
Stuck: Poems Midlife

866-840-4334
http://www.timebeing.com

NORBERT KRAPF
Somewhere in Southern Indiana: Poems of Midwestern Origins
Blue-Eyed Grass: Poems of Germany
Looking for God's Country

ADRIAN C. LOUIS
Blood Thirsty Savages

LEO LUKE MARCELLO
Nothing Grows in One Place Forever: Poems of a Sicilian American

GARDNER McFALL
The Pilot's Daughter

JOSEPH MEREDITH
Hunter's Moon: Poems from Boyhood to Manhood

BEN MILDER
The Good Book Says . . . : Light Verse to Illuminate the Old Testament
The Good Book Also Says . . . : Numerous Humorous Poems Inspired by the
 New Testament
Love Is Funny, Love Is Sad
The Zoo You Never Gnu: A Mad Menagerie of Bizarre Beasts and Birds

CHARLES MUÑOZ
Fragments of a Myth: Modern Poems on Ancient Themes

MICHAEL O'SIADHAIL
The Gossamer Wall: Poems in Witness to the Holocaust